Our San Antonio

Text by Susanna Nawrocki & Gerald Lair
Photography by Mark Langford
Foreword by Claude Stanush

Voyageur Press

First published in 1992. This edition published in 2008 by Voyageur Press, an imprint of MBI Publishing Company LLC, Galtier Plaza, Suite 200, 380 Jackson Street, St. Paul, MN 55101 USA

The information in this book is true and complete to the best of our knowledge. All recommendations are made without any guarantee on the part of the author or Publisher, who also disclaim any liability incurred in connection with the use of this data or specific details.

We recognize, further, that some words, model names, and designations mentioned herein are the property of the trademark holder. We use them for identification purposes only. This is not an official publication.

Voyageur Press titles are also available at discounts in bulk quantity for industrial or sales-promotional use. For details write to Special Sales Manager at MBI Publishing Company, Galtier Plaza, Suite 200, 380 Jackson Street, St. Paul, MN 55101 USA.

To find out more about our books, join us online at www.voyageurpress.com.

Editor: Leah Noel
Designer: Melissa Khaira

Library of Congress Cataloging-in-Publication Data

Nawrocki, Susanna, 1938-

 Our San Antonio/text by Susanna Nawrocki & Gerald Lair; photography by Mark Langford; foreword by Claude Stanush.

   p. cm.

 ISBN-13: 978-0-7603-2973-3 (plc w/ jacket)

 ISBN-10: 0-7603-2973-7 (plc w/ jacket)

 1. San Antonio (Tex.)—Pictorial works. 2. San Antonio (Tex.)—Description and travel. I. Lair, Gerald, 1947- II. Langford, Mark, 1957- III. Title.

F394.S21143N39 2008

976.4'35100222--dc22

2007030867

FRONTIS PAGE: *The intricate rose window, as well as much of the work on the facade of San José, has been attributed to Pedro Huizar, a talented young stone carver who lived at the mission with his wife and family in the 1700s. The design of the rose window appears now and again around San Antonio, outlining the display windows at the Rivercenter Dillard's Department Store and providing the shape for a lily pond at the McNay Art Museum.*

ON THE TITLE PAGE: *The development of San Antonio's famous River Walk began in 1938, seventeen years after a flood caused heavy damage to large portions of the city's downtown sector. The area was invisioned by a young architect, Robert H. H. Hugman, who was from the Alamo City.*

ON THE TITLE PAGE, INSET: *A bell in the pierced three-bell tower at San Antonio's Mission Espada.*

ON THE CONTENTS PAGE: *Summer dance performances at the Arneson River Theatre capture the flavor and passion of Old San Antonio and its cultural roots in Mexico and Spain.*

Contents

First-time visitors to San Antonio are nearly always surprised by what they see. Many have a vision, derived from motion pictures, of a city set in desert country, bare and sun-browned—but once they arrive, they are delighted by the lushness and greenery. Many have a movie-inspired image of the Alamo as a solitary stone fort set somewhere on an open prairie. A recent visitor from San Francisco couldn't believe his eyes when he stepped out of the Hyatt Regency hotel at nighttime and saw that famous citadel of liberty in the heart of downtown, its white walls luminous and magical under a focus of floodlights. Most visitors have heard of San Antonio as one of America's four unique cities, yet they are nearly always surprised at how unique it really is, in almost every way.

When asked to write the foreword for this book about San Antonio, I was surprised, too. Guidebooks are useful for finding your way around cities, but they usually give only a sketchy view of a city's history and even less about the life and character of its citizens. What attracted me about *Our San Antonio* is that it not only tells tourists what to see and experience in this unusual city, it also tells San Antonians things about their city and themselves that will both surprise and enlighten them.

As a native of San Antonio who has lived in several other cities, I have heard San Antonio's alluring call. This city, known as the soul or mother of Texas, has a way of capturing visitors and enticing them to stay.

When the Spaniards came to Texas in the late seventeenth century, it was the San Antonio River (then called Yanaguana by the Indians living in the area) and the springs at its source (still flowing behind the University of the Incarnate Word) that made them settle here. At the center of this first settlement was a *presidio*, or military installation (now Military Plaza with our city hall in the center), and five Roman Catholic missions built at intervals along the river to convert and civilize the nomadic Indians of South Texas. What is a surprise, even to many San Antonians, is that the Alamo originally was not a fort but was one of these missions.

Visitors confused by the city's winding streets often ask whether they were laid out on cow trails or by drunken citizens trying to find their way home. The answer is more logical. The first settlers were given narrow strips of land stretching back from the river from which they drew water to drink and to irrigate their crops. The early roads connecting the narrow strips of land necessarily followed the meandering course of the river, and eventually became the city's streets. That river now winds through San Antonio's downtown and is one of the city's most charming features. Locals as well as tourists love the cobblestone walks along the riverbanks, the shops and restaurants, and the Parisian atmosphere.

My great-grandparents and grandparents came to San Antonio from Poland in the post–Civil War period to escape Europe's recurring wars and to find opportunities denied them in the old country. Other immigrants—from Germany, Czechoslovakia, Ireland, and Italy—came here for similar reasons. These early immigrants naturally settled in little enclaves where they could still speak their own languages and continue the customs they brought with them from their native lands. In the various ethnic enclaves of San Antonio, people tended to keep to themselves, sometimes resenting members of other ethnic groups.

OPPOSITE PAGE: *Originally founded in 1716 in eastern Texas, Mission San Juan Capistrano was transferred in 1731 to its present location. In 1756, the stone church, a friary, and a granary were completed. Currently the National Park Service administers the four missions of the San Antonio Missions Historical Park, while the Daughters of the Republic of Texas have responsibility for the maintenance and exhibits of Mission San Antonio de Valero, better known as the Alamo.*

Young mariachis entertain from a float in the annual King William parade. A popular Fiesta event, the King William parade and fair are traditionally held on the final Saturday of Fiesta Week. Food and craft booths line the streets of this historic neighborhood with games and activities for children and an emphasis on all things local.

In 1968, San Antonio hosted the World's Fair. HemisFair, with its slogan "The Confluence of Cultures," placed emphasis on the positive contributions of the more than thirty-two ethnic groups in San Antonio and did much to overcome negative feelings between groups. Even more so, the creation of the Institute of Texan Cultures during HemisFair provided a common meeting ground for the city's ethnic groups, engendering a mutual respect that has been enhanced by the institute's annual Texas Folklife Festival.

San Antonio represents a confluence of cultures in another important way—it is the nexus of three very different geophysical regions. If you fly from Dallas to San Antonio, you can distinctly see the Balcones Fault, which divides East Texas, with its more abundant rainfall, farms, and forests, from West Texas, with its scant rainfall, scrubby brush, and vast ranches. South of San Antonio is a third geographic area, the Brush Country, which fades off into the coastal plains and the Gulf of Mexico to the east and the country of Mexico to the southwest.

These three geographical areas determine and define three distinct cultures meeting in San Antonio. The city is as far north as the Hispanic-Mexican culture advanced before it was halted by the Comanche Indians in the eighteenth and nineteenth centuries; as far west as the Southern culture came with its cotton plantations, Southern cuisine, and folkways; and as far east as the open-range cattle kingdom came, with its cowboy, ranch, and horse culture.

Even though Texas won its independence from Mexico in 1836, San Antonio has never given up its early Mexican culture. Today the city's population is more than 50 percent Hispanic. You can hear Spanish spoken on radio, TV, and almost any street corner, and you can see it on signs and advertisements. The Mexican national holidays of Cinco de Mayo and Diez y Seis are celebrated, Mexican food is the dominant cuisine, and almost every celebration includes Mexican mariachis or conjunto music. Mexican architecture is seen everywhere, particularly in red-tile roofs and saltillo tile floors.

When the Comanches halted the Hispanic-Mexican movement north, the government in Mexico City invited American settlers into the Texas province to bolster its defenses. Many came from the southern states through Louisiana, and their culture is seen in San Antonio's Greek Revival architecture, the local taste for smoked ham and hush puppies, organizations like the Texas Cavaliers, the queen and duchesses of the annual Fiesta celebrations, and remnant rebel drawls and attitudes.

Ranch and cowboy culture came to Texas from Mexico and then spread to the rest of the United States from San Antonio and the Brush Country. When I was a kid, my family had a ranch near Pleasanton (about thirty-five miles south of San Antonio) that we believe was part of Mission San José's Rancho del Atascosa, one of the very first ranches in Texas and in the United States.

In the center of Pleasanton is a statue of a cowboy claiming this is where the American ranching industry was born. The Spaniards brought their longhorn cattle and their *vaqueros* (the forerunners of American cowboys) to this region from Mexico; later, after the Civil War, Texas cowboys not only drove Texas longhorns to railroads in Kansas to supply the eastern states with beef, but drove them to nearly all of the western states to provide seed stock for the great American ranching industry.

On our ranch was an old bowlegged cowboy, Alex Morose, who had driven cattle up the trail when he was only fourteen or fifteen years old. He slept on the wooden floor of his room because he had slept outside so long that he never got used to sleeping in a bed. San Antonio was the headquarters city for many of those old trail drivers, and their annual conventions were held in the Gunter Hotel. Today, there is a museum next to the Witte Museum in Brackenridge Park that is devoted to trail drivers. It tells their history and exhibits their clothing and equipment, six-shooters, and rifles—but the legendary ten-gallon hat, leather or canvas jacket, and leather chaps and gauntlets of the cowboy were not designed for show; they were worn for protection against the dense, thorny chaparral of the Brush Country.

Flags of many countries line the plaza between UTSA's Institute of Texan Cultures and the Tower of the Americas in celebration of Texas' cultural heritage.

The old-time cowboys may be gone now, but their culture is still strong in San Antonio. I hardly know anybody here, with or without money, who doesn't have a secret yearning to own a ranch. Young and old love to wear cowboy hats, boots, and big belt buckles. Ranching clothes come out of the closet during the annual San Antonio Stock Show and Rodeo each February. And what would a typical Texas meal be without barbecue and beans?

The juncture of the three geographical zones makes San Antonio a unique city in still another way. Its flora and fauna represent all three regions; here you find Southern pines, magnolias, and azaleas; dry-country yuccas, cacti, and palms; and tropical red-flowered hibiscus. The area is a paradise for bird lovers, with Texas boasting the largest variety of species of any state in the country—more than six hundred—a large percentage of which can be seen in San Antonio at one time or another. Countless species of butterflies live here most of the year, while others pass through in migration north or south. One day, on the Guadalupe River north of San Antonio, my wife and I saw a big cypress tree aflutter with as many migrating monarch butterflies as leaves.

Finally, what makes San Antonio so different from most other cities is its authenticity, reflected in its architecture, celebrations, and daily life. The Alamo was not put up for show. Its solid look and its nicked, weathered walls tell you that it stood for something. It is this very character that makes it Texas' most popular tourist attraction. The charm of the other downtown buildings and the River Walk (which continues to be enhanced and extended) has grown out of the city's history and the concern for beauty and authenticity held by its citizens and the San Antonio Conservation Society. Even the details of the buildings—the carved stone, the wrought iron, the intricate woodwork—came out of the skills and sweat of the many craftspeople who arrived as immigrants and then settled here for good. Various vested interests greedy for tourist dollars have done their best to put a shiny veneer over the city's authenticity, but citizens have consistently fought such efforts. It is still true that what is most attractive to people about San Antonio, to citizens and tourists alike, is that most of what you see here is for real.

With industrialization, of course, fewer and fewer San Antonians are doing old-time handiwork and crafts. But the various traditions have been continued at the Southwest School of Art and Craft, housed in the old limestone-walled Ursuline Convent where my mother went to school as a young girl. The city also has a long tradition of fine art. From the time of Texas' independence on, San Antonio's natural beauty and exotic character made it especially attractive to artists of all kinds— painters, sculptors, potters, and writers. Like the immigrant craftspeople, the early artists came mostly from Europe, but they came primarily from the upper classes and were trained in some of Europe's best art schools. Their documentation of San Antonio in its various stages of development now gives us a deepened sense of our history as well as a historical appreciation for art that continues in our fine, world-class museums—like the McNay Art Museum and the San Antonio Museum of Art— and in the many artists who reside here. The aesthetic sense, along with the city's diversity and reputation for friendliness and love of celebration, have created something called "the San Antonio style" that is different from that of any other city.

But if San Antonio's past is rich, what about its future? Can the city prosper in an increasingly competitive, high-tech world economy when, unfortunately, a significant portion of our population is undereducated and underemployed?

Although this will be a growing challenge, the outlook in key areas—from big business to medical care and scientific research to the arts—looks bright. Historically, tourism and the military have been economic mainstays for San Antonio, and although tourism remains strong, the military presence has declined. In the meantime, however, the city's health care and bio-science industry has grown, buttressed by long-tenured institutions such as The Southwest Foundation for Biomedical Research and the South Texas Medical Center. In the business arena, San Antonio is the national headquarters for

The annual San Antonio Stock Show and Rodeo is held every February for two weeks. Festivities include rodeos, music, livestock competitions, a midway, and family fun, starting with trail rides entering the city from all directions and the very early morning cowboy breakfast.

telecommunication giant AT&T, and innovative auto manufacturing company Toyota has invested $800 million in a truck assembly plant here. Washington Mutual, a national financial services leader, has also picked the city for a huge regional operations center. And San Antonio's proximity to Mexico continues to make it a natural gateway for trade with that country.

In the arts arena, all kinds of ventures are sprouting or growing, including the Blue Star Arts Complex, a contemporary arts incubator built in an old warehouse district; ArtPace, which brings contemporary artists to San Antonio from all over the globe; the Smithsonian-affiliated Museo Alameda at Market Square; and a $9.3 million Asian art wing at the ever-expanding San Antonio Museum of Art. Indeed, Marion Oettinger, director of the SAMA, says that in his more than twenty years in the city he has never seen so many things happening at once. "We have arrived at a critical mass of talent, a positive economy, and visionary leadership—all of these things just seem to be coming together," he says.

Realizing that a modern, competitive economy has to be a creative economy, our city leaders are increasing support for our many art organizations and planning other projects that promise to attract creative individuals and companies that operate on the cutting edge. For those who love sports, there is the pro basketball team, the San Antonio Spurs, which has won multiple NBA championships.

When I left San Antonio at the age of twenty-six to become a correspondent and writer for *Life* magazine, I wondered if I would ever return. In the intervening years, I traveled all over the world and saw many fabulous cities. Eventually, though, I had that yearning to move back to the city that I knew and came to love as a boy. When I met my wife, Barbara, I was living in New York, and as a couple we continued to live there, though we often visited my mother in San Antonio. After one such visit, we asked each other the same question: "What would you think of moving to San Antonio?"

New York was an exciting place to live; we both loved the theater and the art galleries and museums. But San Antonio was growing and becoming more cosmopolitan, and we felt in the flux of life there as much as in New York, perhaps more so because of better opportunities for connecting more personally with people of many different occupations. Neither of us hesitated. "Let's go," we answered at the same time. We have never regretted it.

— Claude Stanush, longtime journalist for *Life* magazine, short story and book author, and Pulitzer Prize nominee

Although the Alamo is known by all as the site where a small band of Texas settlers stood their ground against the Mexican army, it was actually built as the first Spanish mission in the San Antonio River Valley.

Introduction

Welcome to San Antonio, the Alamo City. Each year, San Antonio embraces, entertains, captivates, and charms not only its own citizens, but also millions of visitors. People come from all over the world because there's much to see, much to do, and much to remember. Experiencing the full measure of what the city has to offer requires a working knowledge of its history and a healthy dose of organization and planning. This book offers a visual and verbal tour of the sights, sounds, events, people, and places that make the Alamo City so special. It's the big picture and more. When writing about San Antonio, the most difficult challenge is figuring out where to begin. So let's start at the top.

From the observation deck atop the 750-foot Tower of the Americas, you truly see San Antonio. On a clear day, the entire city is in view, as is a varied and picturesque countryside—a patchwork of mostly flat farm and ranchlands to the south and east, gently rolling hills due north, and the fabled Texas Hill Country to the west. Straight down is HemisFair Park, ninety-two acres of redeveloped land that was once the home of HemisFair '68, San Antonio's World's Fair.

This vantage point gives you the opportunity not only to see, but also to feel the magnificence of a proud place deemed as "one of America's four unique cities," where skyscrapers engulf bricked streets, a shopping mall surrounds a church, the San Antonio River meanders through the central city with its legendary cobblestone River Walk, the Alamo rests in quiet solitude, and Market Square brims with activity as people shop and dine and trolleys ding as they go. San Antonio is a romantic setting, complete with the indelible charm of La Villita (the little village along the river), the elegance of the ageless Menger Hotel, the tranquility of a horse-drawn carriage ride, and a rich past evidenced by the missions of San José, San Juan Capistrano, Concepción, and San Francisco de la Espada. A confluence of cultures makes San Antonio great.

From your cloudlike perch, you'll see the German-influenced King William Historic District, the French architecture of the old Ursuline Academy that is now the Southwest School of Art and Craft, the Spanish character of the Spanish Governor's Palace, and the eight-sided neo-Gothic design of the Tower Life Building—a thirty-one-story edifice that was the South's tallest structure when built in the late 1920s. You'll even gaze at river revelers floating on barges, the hustle and bustle of conventioneers around the Henry B. Gonzalez Convention Center, and an internationally famous zoo. From high above the cityscape, pick out Sea World of Texas, Six Flags Fiesta Texas, three important military installations, the Alamodome, and the AT&T Center, home of the San Antonio Spurs. You'll also get a bird's-eye view of lush greenbelts and over seventy-five city parks that feature a myriad of tree species, including oak, mesquite, cypress, willow, elm, hackberry, mulberry, huisache, persimmon, and pecan. San Antonio's warm, sunbelt climate supports a preponderance of plant life, creating a vivid kaleidoscope of color in the overall beauty of the city below.

Once back on the ground, it's time to immerse yourself in the traditions and passions of the Alamo City. Although the celebration we call Fiesta San Antonio is officially in April of each year, San Antonio is really a fiesta every day. The food alone is enough to get you fired up. A visit is not complete without Mexican food, margaritas, and mariachis. Bite into a jalapeno, buy a sombrero, barge in on a river taxi, and be happy. This is San Antonio—alluring and unique. The experience is exceptional. San Antonio casts a spell.

OPPOSITE PAGE: *The 750-foot Tower of the Americas, shown here bathed in fireworks, is the enduring symbol of HemisFair '68, San Antonio's World's Fair. The tower features a restaurant that revolves 360 degrees, an observation deck with a bird's-eye view of the city, and a Texas-themed, 4-D multisensory theater.*

At one time, the San Antonio Convention and Visitor's Bureau used the promotional theme, "Nowhere else but San Antonio." The Spanish translation for this is *"Solamente en San Antonio."* The phrase truly captured the Alamo City's one-of-a-kind nature. Although no longer the official slogan for the city, it still speaks volumes today. Sample a snow cone on the street; find a festival any time of the year; applaud an armadillo race; chase down prize-winning chili with an ice-cold cerveza; or maybe even saunter on over to the Majestic for a symphony, a Broadway play, or an outstanding performance by a nationally known celebrity. San Antonio has something for everyone, at the drop of a hat. But most of all, San Antonio has character. We cherish our past, live our present to the fullest, and anticipate a bright and successful future.

The San Antonio metropolitan area encompasses a population of almost one and a half million people. About half of the residents are of Hispanic descent, about seven percent are African-American, a small percentage are Asian and other ethnicities, with the remainder being melting-pot Anglo. We all live together, work together, and enjoy San Antonio together. The city offers a diverse workplace, from manufacturing to military, retail to livestock, tourism to petroleum production, banking to medicine, and just about everything in between.

The first European visitors came to what is now San Antonio over three hundred years ago. The rest is history. In the pages that follow, you are invited to enjoy an overview of the important people, places, and things that shaped our city.

Fiesta Noche del Rio, a celebration of Mexican song and dance, takes the stage at the Arneson River Theatre each year from May to August. The tradition began in 1957.

OPPOSITE PAGE: *La Mansion del Rio Hotel was one of several downtown lodging facilities built for HemisFair '68. Located on the famed San Antonio River Walk, this highly rated hotel features exceptional Spanish colonial architecture, 338 rooms and suites, lush courtyards, and the award-winning Las Canarias Restaurant.*

Fiesta San Antonio is a ten-day citywide celebration held annually in April. It is one of the nation's premiere festivals with over 100 events, including parades, concerts, art shows, and a wide variety of food and drink gatherings. The women shown here reflect the heritage and spirit of Fiesta San Antonio.

Historic Market Square in the downtown area is composed of three areas: Produce Row (shops and restaurants), El Mercado (shops in a large Mexico-styled market), and Farmer's Market (shops and a food court). Market Square is a favorite of visitors and locals alike and features live music and lively events almost every weekend.

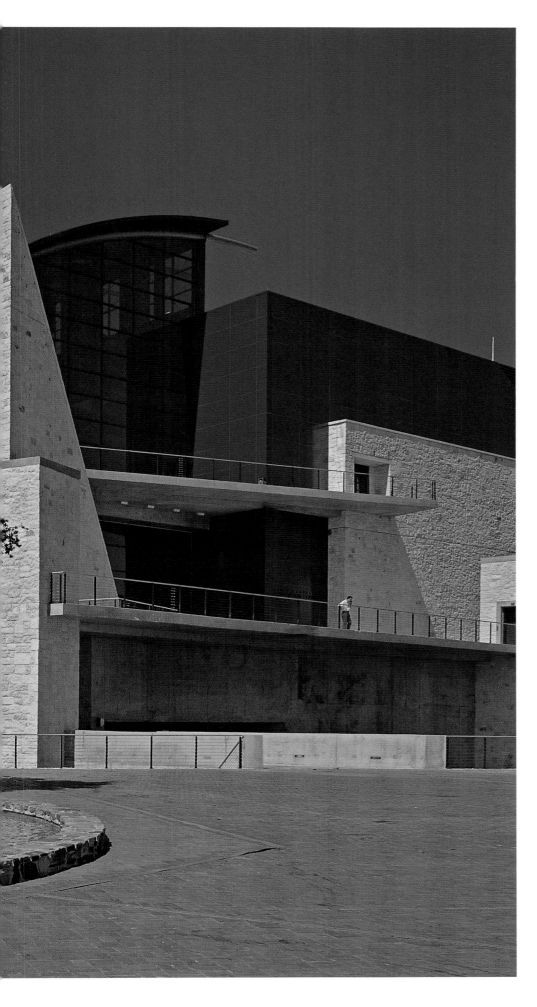

The Henry B. Gonzalez Convention Center, named after the first Hispanic elected to the U.S. House of Representatives, opened with HemisFair '68 on April 6, 1968. In recent years, the center has been greatly expanded and now boasts 1.3 million square feet of meeting space.

The traditional Mexican piñata is a six-point star like the one shown in this photograph. However, countless other shapes are available as well. Crafted from paper, piñatas are filled with wrapped candy. Traditionally they are dangled from trees where blindfolded children strike them with sticks, eventually releasing treats for all to enjoy.

OPPOSITE PAGE: *The San Antonio Charro Association has preserved the tradition of Mexican rodeo, also know as Charreada. Charreadas are held from March through October, including two during Fiesta San Antonio, at the association's Charro Ranch on the city's south side.*

The Spanish missions of South Texas were constructed by the first European settlers to enter the area—Spaniards arriving by way of Mexico in the early 1700s. The missions were an essential part of the Spanish blueprint for securing the American Southwest and an important civilizing and economic influence on the raw frontier.

Five of these eighteenth-century missions form a chain that stretches south along the San Antonio River for ten miles. From the Alamo, located in downtown San Antonio and originally known as Mission San Antonio de Valero, to Mission San Francisco de la Espada, lying on the city's southern boundary, the surviving mission structures testify impressively to Spain's attempt to extend its cultural and political hold over the vast areas of New Spain north of the Rio Grande.

Since 1978, four of these missions—Mission Nuestra Señora de la Purisma Concepción de Acuña (Concepción), Mission San José y San Miguel de Aguayo (San José), Mission San Juan Capistrano (San Juan), and Mission San Francisco de la Espada (Espada), along with farmlands that are being acquired when available—have constituted the San Antonio Missions National Park. (The fifth mission, known today as the Alamo, is administered by the Daughters of the Republic of Texas.) Rangers are on duty at each location along the 7 ½-mile–long Mission Hike and Bike Trail between these missions to answer questions. The Catholic parishes that worship at each of the four mission churches celebrate mass on a regular basis and welcome visitors.

One hundred years ago, a visit to missions Espada and San Juan, ten miles from the city center, meant an overnight trip. Today, you can easily explore the four national park missions in a day by following Mission Parkway as it winds south from Mission Concepción. When completed, the San Antonio Mission Hike and Bike Trail, a paved two-lane road designed for auto, foot, and bicycle traffic and often running parallel to the San Antonio River, will connect all of San Antonio's missions from the Alamo to Mission Espada. Pick up a map of the route at Concepción or at the San Antonio Missions National Historic Park Headquarters, 2202 Roosevelt Avenue, or hop aboard one of the tour buses leaving from Alamo Plaza.

But before you do, first learn a little history about these beautiful structures.

While the thirteen colonies on North America's eastern seaboard were gearing up for and fighting the American Revolution, Franciscan priests, Spanish soldier-settlers from northern Mexico, mission Indians, and a small band of settlers from the Canary Islands were struggling to wrest communities from the sometimes hospitable, often barren and hostile, frontier of New Spain—the area we know today as South Texas.

When Domingo Terán de los Rios, an explorer and the first governor of this area, passed through the San Antonio River Valley in 1691 on his way to visit Spain's missions in East Texas, he noted the fine, well-watered country and visualized the valley as an ideal location for a new mission. A community midway between East Texas and the Rio Grande would serve as a convenient stopover for supply caravans traveling to the East Texas missions.

In the late 1600s, Spain's concern that the French, who held Louisiana, might make inroads into New Spain along the Gulf Coast or across the Sabine River led to the establishment of missions in East Texas. However, it was not until 1718,

OPPOSITE PAGE: *Mission Espada, formally known as San Francisco de la Espada (Saint Francis of the Sword), is one of the three missions relocated from East Texas in 1731. Upon relocation, the word "Espada" was added to the mission's name for reasons unknown today, though some believe that the upraised hand of the altar figure of Saint Francis at one time held an espada, or sword.*

twenty-seven years after Terán's visit, that the first mission, San Antonio de Valero, was located in the San Antonio area. Mission San José followed in 1720, and in 1731 the remaining three missions (Concepción, San Juan, and Espada) were relocated from East Texas.

Spain had long used the mission system to advance its culture and to control native peoples while the missionaries converted them to Christianity. The Spanish crown provided funding and protection in the form of forts, or presidios. The one or two friars at each mission served not only as spiritual leaders, but also as educators, architectural advisors, contractors, and labor bosses. They recruited the native peoples, converting them to Christianity and teaching them the Spanish language and rules of "civilized" behavior. At the same time, priests and

The inverted stones at the base of Mission Espada's doorway arch give the doorway a puzzling and somewhat Moorish shape. To the left stands a wooden cross reputed to have been carried about the grounds as the congregation prayed for rain during a severe drought around 1870. The rains came, and Father Bouchu instructed the parishioners to place the cross by the door as a reminder of the power of prayer.

natives worked together to design and construct the extensive mission compounds.

The mission Indians came from an aggregate of tribes known as Coahuiltecans, hunter-gatherers who subsisted in the mild South Texas climate on fruits, nuts, beans, seeds, and occasional game and fish. Protection from attack by the Lipan Apaches to the north, as well as the promise of a constant food supply, made mission life attractive to these peaceful peoples. However, the tradeoffs required by the rigid organization of mission life often led them to return to their nomadic existence where the rhythms of nature rather than the sound of hourly bells defined their day.

Though the mission period drew to a close in the early 1800s, the legacy of Spain and the mission Indians can be seen today not only in the historic buildings, but also in irrigation practices, ranching equipment and techniques, law, architecture, and language.

The first, or northernmost, mission along Mission Parkway is Nuestra Señora de la Purisma Concepción de Acuña (Mission Concepción), located just east of the confluence of San Pedro Creek and the San Antonio River. A map will show you that the Spanish padres were mindful of the availability of water for both the mission compounds and the outlying fields. However, trial and error, as well as common sense and luck, were required to avoid settling in the flood plain. Both San Antonio de Valero and San José missions were moved several times before safe locations were secured.

As you approach the facade of Mission Concepción, notice the distinctive triangle above the door matched by pyramid shapes atop each bell tower. This geometric simplicity was originally enlivened by painted quatrefoils and squares of red, blue, and yellow—Moorish designs thought to appeal to the Indians. The colors remained vivid as late as 1890, but have since weathered to faint traces.

The mission compound at Concepción is no longer in existence, but the church itself looks much as it did two hundred years ago. Constructed of adobe and a light, porous limestone quarried nearby, it is thought to be the oldest unreconstructed and still-intact church in America. Fortunately, it survived its stint as a troop barracks and cattle pen during the mid-1800s.

The exterior of the mission is Spanish Colonial in style, and the interior follows traditional European cathedral design—a vaulted cruciform shape with baptistry and bell room on either side of the entrance door and a dome topped by a small cupola above the intersection of the arms of the cruciform. The small, vaulted chapels, located at the base of each bell tower, were once covered with splendid murals, but now only patchy fragments remain. Many find this church to be the most beautifully proportioned of all the mission churches. The nave is noted for its fine acoustics.

Continue along Mission Parkway for about three miles to the next mission: San José y San Miguel de Aguayo. It was established in 1720 by Father Antonio Margil, a priest from the East Texas missions who found the San Antonio area to his liking and petitioned the authorities in Mexico for permission to relocate here.

The most extensively renovated of all the sites, San José will provide you with a window into the order, security, and austere beauty the padres sought to create in the midst of a bountiful but chaotic wilderness.

An award-winning twenty-minute film in the San José visitor's center provides a fine introduction to the history of the San Antonio missions and illustrates what typical mission life would have been like. Daily chores were governed by routines as predictable and symmetrical as the mission architecture. Rations were issued on certain days, and the passage of the day was marked by the ringing of mission bells to signal changes of activity from dawn to nightfall.

San José's thick stone walls, reinforced on the interior by the workshops and living quarters, enclosed a perfectly square compound 611 feet long on each side, with facilities serving all the needs of the community—workshops for weavers, carpenters, and blacksmiths; a sugar mill for making cane syrup and

This sculpture of San Joaquin, located on the north side of the entrance doors at San José Mission, was restored by Ernest Lenarduzzi in the late 1940s. San Joaquin was the husband of Saint Anne, the mother of the Virgin Mary, whose figure can be found on the opposite side of the entrance.

brown sugar bars; a water supply; storage facilities; a granary; and a convent with offices for the priests.

The church itself—with its carved stonework and wooden doors, spare but beautiful interior, and solid oak circular stairway to the bell tower—is a monument to artisanship and ingenuity. A priest who visited the mission in the eighteenth century, Friar Juan Morfi, wrote, "This building, because of its size, good taste, and beauty, would grace a large city as a parish church."

In addition to the enclosed compounds and surrounding fields, each mission operated a livestock facility some miles distant. The San José ranch, El Atascosa, was located to the

29

The elaborate, much-restored facade of the church at Mission San José features statues of a number of saints, including San José (Saint Joseph) and the Virgin of Guadalupe, patroness of Mexico. The saints are surrounded by intricate carvings of religious designs and symbols. Carved cedar doors, replicas of the originals that were stolen in the 1880s, open into a sanctuary of contrasting simplicity and stately beauty.

south of San José. At times, it had as many as three thousand head each of cattle and sheep, one hundred horses for *vaqueros* and shepherds, eighty mares, and thirty yoke of oxen.

When Friar Gaspar José Solis stopped at Rancho del Atascosa in 1768, he wrote that the ranch was entirely operated by mission Indians with no Spanish overseer—testimony to the innate abilities of the native Coahuiltecans and the training and organizational skills of the priests, as well as to the scarcity of priests and soldiers. Though the use of horses in New Spain remained the exclusive privilege of the Spanish *cabelleros*, the gentlemen of the Spanish haciendas, this rule was overlooked on the frontier. For the native *vaquero*, forerunner of the American cowboy, the horse was the mainstay of daily work.

About a mile down the parkway from Mission San José, you'll come to Espada Park and the oldest existing dam in the

United States. Espada Dam is of interest from an engineering standpoint because, unlike in most dams, the walls curve downstream with the flow of the water. Built to divert water from the San Antonio River into an acequia that irrigated the crops in the Espada fields, it has survived for over 260 years. Due to flood control measures taken in the 1950s, the main river channel now bypasses Espada Dam. The dam and its water level, however, have been carefully preserved.

With the unpredictable rainfall and hot, dry summers of South Texas, the mission irrigation systems were a high priority. Based on the *acequia*—a Spanish word from the Arabic *as-sāqiyah* meaning "irrigation stream"—the system, originally developed by the Moors for the arid regions of Spain, was easily adapted to the American Southwest and served to ensure a plentiful supply of water and, therefore, food.

One of the earliest examples of planned water use in North America, *acequias* were employed by the *villa* (town) and *presidio* (fort) as well; at one time seven *acequias* drew from the waters of San Pedro Creek and the San Antonio River. Strict rules prohibited the use of irrigation ditches for laundry or trash disposal. This fifteen-mile network, which included five dams and at least two aqueducts, irrigated nearly thirty-five hundred acres of land.

The Espada system, including Espada Aqueduct, which carries the acequia waters over Piedras Creek, still flows today and is considered the oldest operational irrigation system in the United States.

The last two missions along the trail, San Juan Capistrano and San Francisco de la Espada, appear small in comparison to San José and have not undergone such extensive renovation. However, San Juan at one time yielded massive quantities of produce—enough to support not only itself but also other local missions, the presidio, and the town, as well as an established trade route to Louisiana and Mexico.

Distinctive belfries at both San Juan and Espada consist of triple arches piercing the flat wall above the chapel doors, each arch designed to hold a bell.

The altar in the chapel at San Juan is flanked by very old statues of Christ and the Virgin Mary. Made of cornstalk pith and coated and painted, they are products of a process perfected by the Indians of central Mexico before the Spanish Conquest. The central figure above the altar is that of San Juan Capistrano, a fifteenth-century theologian for whom the mission was named.

Noteworthy today at Espada is the chapel (rebuilt in 1868) with its unusual Moorish door. Observe that the stones at the base of the arch have been reversed, causing a break in the line of the arch. Whether this unusual configuration occurred by accident or by design is unknown.

Espada, in danger of disappearing completely during the 1800s, was rescued by a twenty-nine-year-old Franciscan, Father François Bouchu, who was so attracted to this place, the most remote of missions, that he took up residence in 1858. For the next forty years, he personally restored much of the old mission, rebuilding the church and adding a wood floor, choir loft, sanctuary railing, and pews. Bouchu is said to have worked on the restoration until a week before his death.

After leaving Mission Espada, follow Espada Road for a mile and a half, looking carefully for historical markers, to see the Espada Aqueduct. Built of a soft and easily quarried limestone that hardens with exposure to air, the Roman arches of the 260-plus-year-old aqueduct support a channel four feet wide and four feet deep that carries irrigation water over Piedras Creek.

The mission system waxed and waned throughout the eighteenth century. Measles, cholera, smallpox, and typhoid devastated the Indian population, which had no resistance to these European diseases. Many tired of the restrictive community life and simply walked away. The Lipan Apaches found the fledgling villas and the Indians working outside the mission walls easy marks for attack. For all these reasons, a thriving second generation of mission Indians never materialized, and new workers had to be continually recruited.

Finally, toward the end of the 1700s, the Spanish government turned to defending itself against revolution from within and began to abandon the missions. In addition, it imposed a tax on mission cattle, which destroyed this means of livelihood. By 1821, Mexico had won its independence from Spain, and by 1824 all the missions had become secular communities. Although some sections of San Juan were rented to Spanish colonists, most mission land, livestock, and movable inventory were parceled out to the remaining Indians.

The mission communities, designed initially to be self-sufficient and totally separate from the villa and the presidio, now merged with those populations. As the nineteenth century began, the community centered between San Pedro Creek and the San Antonio River had become an amalgam of Canary Islanders, mission Indians, and residents from the presidio.

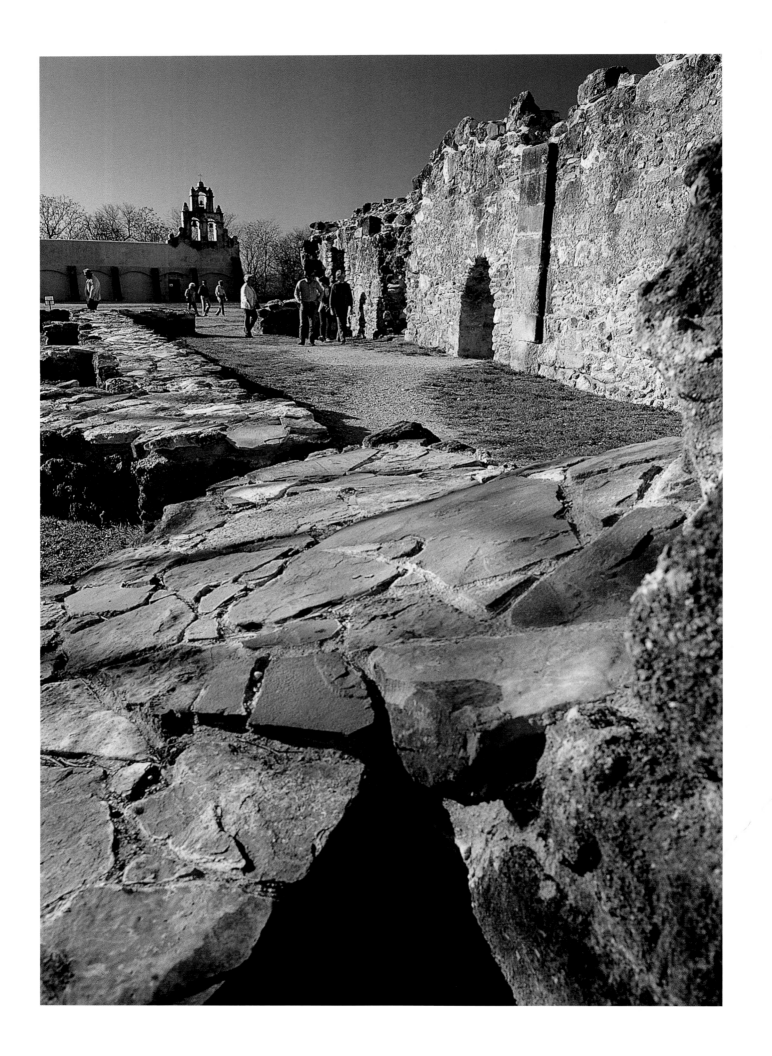

The mission buildings themselves began to crumble. Visitors in 1890, one hundred years after secularization, might have sent their friends a postcard showing the weed-covered ruins of San José with the inscription "The Mission, between the elements and the festive vandal, will soon be no more."

Today, thanks to Los Compadres (Friends of the Missions), the San Antonio Conservation Society, the National Park Service, the Archdiocese of San Antonio, and the parish communities, as well as the many individuals in San Antonio who care about the preservation of the missions, the San Antonio missions have not succumbed to the "elements and the festive vandal." Instead, they stand as centerpieces of the history of San Antonio and the Southwest.

ABOVE: *A metal flower design graces the door at Mission San Juan de Capistrano.*

LEFT: *The church at Mission Concepción was dedicated in 1755 and has changed little since that time. The least restored of all the missions, it is a fine example of Spanish Colonial architecture. The builders incorporated elements of Moorish design along with Native American aspects to appeal to their subjects.*

OPPOSITE PAGE: *Records indicate that the chapel at Mission San Juan Capistrano was to have been replaced by a larger, grander church. However, only the foundation of this replacement remains—across the quadrangle from the chapel.*

OPPOSITE PAGE: *The setting sun pierces the belfry of San Juan Capistrano, outlining the delicate bell tower, which has remained intact for over two hundred years.*

LEFT: *Each Sunday at Mission San José, a group of mariachi musicians assists in celebrating the noon mass. Following the service, the congregation follows the mariachis to an area behind the church where young dancers in traditional dress perform for parishioners and visitors.*

The seventy-five-foot bell tower of the San José Church, rebuilt after its collapse in 1930, rises above the tree line just off Mission Road. The rounded shape to the right of the tower contains a circular stairway leading to the bell room and choir loft. The hand-hewn steps of the spiral staircase are held together without nails or pegs; in the 1920s, these solid-oak blocks were found scattered about the grounds and were carefully restored and reassembled to their original configuration.

Afternoon sunlight illuminates a statue of the Virgin Mary to the left of the main altar in San José Mission Church.

The interior of Mission San José has been completely rebuilt. A photo from the turn of the twentieth century shows the sanctuary open to the sky with only the sacristy and bell tower remaining. Fortunately, the San Antonio Conservation Society took an active interest in the mission and in 1924 began to generate the funds, interest, and effort required to preserve the site for future generations.

OPPOSITE PAGE: *The distinctive three-bell espadana (bell tower) of Mission Espada appears today just as it did when completed in 1756.*

Known worldwide as "the cradle of Texas liberty," the Alamo, to the surprise of first-time visitors, is nestled quietly in downtown San Antonio, its walled gardens a pleasant respite from the city life that swirls around it.

Much of the famous battle, in which more than 180 Texans and Americans suffered defeat and death at the hands of the army of Antonio López de Santa Anna in March 1836, took place between the church and South Alamo Street, where Alamo Plaza lies today. Part of the original west wall of the Alamo grounds can be seen at the entrance to the Paseo del Alamo, which leads from Alamo Plaza to the River Walk.

The Alamo is best known, of course, as the site of the bloody battle between Mexicans and Texas settlers, but it began its existence as the first Spanish mission in the San Antonio River Valley. Officially founded in 1718, Mission San Antonio de Valero was not settled in its present location until six years later. Historians suspect that the first location lay to the west of San Pedro Creek near the present-day intersection of North Salado and Laredo streets.

A year after the founding, Father Antonio Olivares, the first priest of the mission, moved it just east of the river bend, about where Saint Joseph's Church stands today. But in 1724, a hurricane destroyed the huts and small stone tower at the second location, and Mission San Antonio de Valero was moved to its final resting place a bit to the north.

If you stood in front of the Alamo today, you would hardly notice the river that passes just a few hundred yards to the west. Yet the river was probably the most important feature of the landscape when Father Olivares chose this location. A desirable site had to be close to water but not prone to flooding. Surrounding fields must be easily irrigated in order to support the mission's agricultural endeavors.

The first task of the mission Indians recruited by Father Olivares was to construct the Alamo Madre ditch, a two-and-a-half-mile *acequia* that carried water for irrigation and drinking from the headwaters of the river—near present-day University of the Incarnate Word at Broadway and Hildebrand avenues—south behind the mission walls and back into the river in the King William area.

In addition to the water system, the mission Indians constructed living quarters, offices for the priests, kitchens, and a dining hall. The convent, part of which later became the Long Barrack (where many Texans and Americans died in the Battle of the Alamo), was originally a two-story building with arches on both floors. It was arranged in a square with an interior courtyard.

Records indicate that the church itself, the construction of which began in 1744, collapsed twice. The original plan probably called for two bell towers, but the builders only completed the facade (which carries the date of 1758) up to the cornices.

Though inspectors described Mission San Antonio de Valero as a thriving community in the mid-1700s, by 1793 the Indian population was in serious decline. Mission San Antonio became the first of the five missions to undergo secularization. The government distributed the mission's rich farmlands along with tools, seeds, houses, and animals to the Indians and shut down the mission. The parish of San Fernando de Bexar took over the religious functions of the mission. By the time of the Texas Revolution (War of Independence) in 1835 and 1836, many involved had no inkling that their fort had once existed as a religious community.

OPPOSITE PAGE: *The annual pilgrimage to the Alamo on the first Monday of Fiesta Week in April commemorates the valiant defense by the Texans. Flowers are laid by participating organizations.*

The Spanish authorities stationed troops from the Mexican town of San José y Santiago del Alamo de Parras at Mission San Antonio de Valero for twelve years, beginning in 1801. The garrison's hometown, Alamo ("cottonwood") de Parras, was so named because of its proximity to a certain cottonwood tree in Coahuila, Mexico. In San Antonio, the name of the garrison was commonly shortened to El Alamo, and over time the troops' quarters themselves became known as El Alamo. Thus, Mission San Antonio de Valero acquired the name that survives into the twenty-first century.

After gaining independence from Spain in 1821, the Mexican government continued to encourage immigration from the United States and Europe as a means of populating what it called the Northern Frontier. Throughout the 1820s, Anglo-Americans joined Stephen F. Austin and other *empresarios* (land agents) who, by permission of the Mexican government, controlled the settlement of vast quantities of land. Other Anglos slipped in unnoticed and claimed a bit of Texas for themselves. In exchange for land, settlers agreed to accept the Mexican constitution and the doctrines of the Roman Catholic Church.

By 1830, the Mexican government had become concerned about the burgeoning numbers of immigrants from the north. Though it had hoped to encourage Europeans and Mexicans to colonize the area, the vast majority were Anglos and their African-American slaves from the American South. These newer Anglos did not assimilate into the Mexican culture as early Anglo immigrants had; instead, they formed their own enclaves, speaking English and retaining their Anglo customs.

In an attempt to counter these trends, Mexico passed a law in 1830 prohibiting further immigration to Mexico from the United States. Earlier it had begun rescinding tax abatements formerly used to encourage immigration to the Northern Frontier. The new law, piled on top of these previous mandates, alarmed settlers, who felt that their land claims were in jeopardy and worried that a highly centralized Mexican government might enforce an 1829 law abolishing slavery.

When Santa Anna became president of Mexico, the movement toward a strong central government seemed unavoidable. Nevertheless, settlers remained divided between those who advocated for pressuring the Mexican government to return to the more favorable Constitution of 1824 and those who leaned toward independence from Mexico. Many Tejanos (Texans of Spanish-Indian ancestry) in San Antonio were dissatisfied with Mexican rule and in the end sided with the Anglo-Americans against Santa Anna, even though this path led to their becoming minority citizens in their own land.

Tensions heightened, and in 1835 Santa Anna sent his brother-in-law, General Martin Perfecto de Cos, to secure San Antonio. All that autumn, the Texans laid siege to San Antonio where General Cos and his eight hundred men were encamped. Cos tore down the arches of the Alamo church on the east side and constructed an earthen ramp so his soldiers could haul cannons to the top of the wall.

Despite Cos' preparations at the Alamo, the final hours of the Siege of Béxar took place not around the fort, but in the streets, plazas, and homes across the river to the west. Ben Milam, former Indian fighter and scout, led the Texan army in five days of hand-to-hand combat against Cos and his forces. Milam himself was one of the four Texans killed that December.

The defeated Cos signed the surrender papers in a house in La Villita, now known as the Cos House. Enraged by this defeat

OPPOSITE PAGE: *The familiar facade of the Alamo had a markedly different appearance in 1836 when the famous battle occurred. At that time, it was complete only to the cornices. The rounded, upper part, designed by architect John Fries, along with a roof and two interior support pillars, were added by the U.S. Army after it leased the building in 1849 for use as a quartermaster depot. Statuary niches on either side of the door were a part of the original church design.*

LEFT: *From Losoya Street in front of the Hyatt Regency Hotel, visitors can look along the Paseo del Alamo, a walkway cut between Alamo Plaza and the San Antonio River, for a dramatic view of the Alamo. In December, the city's official Christmas tree appears to dwarf the ancient mission-fort.*

RIGHT: *In the stillness of early morning, you can almost hear the echo of cannons at the Alamo grounds.*

of the Mexican forces, Santa Anna vowed to eradicate resistance in San Antonio, which consisted of fewer than two thousand citizens.

In late February 1836, Santa Anna and his four thousand troops attacked the Texan forces. Although they received word that the Mexican army had crossed the Rio Grande with a large force, they did not expect Santa Anna to cover the intervening brushland so quickly.

The Texans fortified the Alamo as best they could, using the earthen mounds and cannons left behind by Cos in the earlier siege. The compound was difficult to guard, however. Only 150 men were available to defend the four acres. On the morning of

February 23, William Travis and James Bowie, joint commanders, moved all their forces to the Alamo compound. Santa Anna entered the city unimpeded, flying the red flag of no quarter from the tower of San Fernando Church on Main Plaza. The Texans answered his demand for surrender with a shot from the Alamo.

On February 24, Travis wrote his famous letter, addressed to the "People of Texas and all Americans in the World," in which he vowed to fight to the death. His request for reinforcements went largely unanswered, with the exception of thirty-two men from Gonzales, a town to the east, who entered the compound on March 1.

Couriers continued to leave and re-enter the Alamo with relative ease, and it appears that the defenders could have orchestrated a nighttime escape many times during the siege. Even though the odds were clearly against them, the soldiers chose to stay and fight.

The final assault occurred at dawn on March 6—thirteen days after the beginning of the siege. It lasted less than two hours. All the defenders were killed, but a few women and children who had taken refuge in the Alamo survived. Santa Anna gave each two dollars and a blanket and let them go to spread word of the massacre to their fellow Texans.

According to the account of Francisco Antonio Ruiz, the Mexicans ordered the bodies of the defenders burned. Ruiz, along with other officials of the city, was commanded to build the enormous pyre and assist in transporting the Mexican dead to their burial ground in a cemetery near today's Christus Santa Rosa Hospital. Ruiz reported that the "gallantry of the few Texans who

defended the Alamo was really wondered at by the Mexican army. Even the generals were astonished at their vigorous resistance and how dearly victory had been bought."

Indeed, Santa Anna lost hundreds of men to the Alamo's 180-plus defenders. Many more members of the Mexican army were incapacitated by wounds. The time it took them to regroup and move out of San Antonio gave Sam Houston and the forces of the newly created Republic of Texas time to prepare for battle. On April 21 at San Jacinto, not far from present-day Houston, the tables were turned. The Texan forces surprised and overwhelmed Santa Anna's army in a brief but decisive battle.

The Alamo lay in ruins for over ten years after the battle. Then, in 1849, the U.S. Army leased it from the Roman Catholic Church as a quartermaster depot for the storage of hay and grain. The army repaired the fort, raised the walls of the church and convent, and added a roof and two windows

LEFT AND ABOVE: *The Menger Hotel opened its doors on Alamo Plaza in 1859 to serve the commercial district growing up around the army's quartermaster depot located in the old Alamo. Its history includes hosting such famous guests as General Robert E. Lee, poet Sidney Lanier, writer O. Henry, and, of course, Teddy Roosevelt, who is said to have recruited his Rough Riders in the famous Menger Bar.*

The cenotaph, with relief figures of the defenders of the Alamo sculpted by local artist Pompeo Coppini, was erected on Alamo Plaza in 1936 to commemorate the one-hundred-year anniversary of the Battle of the Alamo. Names of the defenders are chiseled into the base, and statues of James Bonham, James Bowie, Davy Crockett, and William Travis are located on each side. The Emily Morgan Hotel can be seen in the background to the right.

to the facade. At this time, the characteristic upper portion of the Alamo facade was designed and added—providing the familiar arched shape that appears in building design all over San Antonio. The army used the chapel as a depot until 1878, when it opened the new Government Hill site, today's Fort Sam Houston.

After serving as a mission, a fort, and a storage depot, the Alamo played a new role in the community in 1878—that of shopping emporium. Honoré Grenet, a merchant of French descent, leased all the grounds except the chapel at a price of $19,000 for ninety-nine years. He built a fortlike structure on top of the barracks and convent, turning them into a

department store containing an ocean of goods of every imaginable description. The Alamo Church became his warehouse. When Grenet died in 1882, Charles Hugo, Gustav Schmeltzer, and William Heuermann, wholesale grocers and liquor dealers, acquired the lease from Grenet's estate and continued to use the old mission for retail purposes.

The chapel itself was sold in 1883 to the state of Texas for $20,000; the state cleaned it out, repaired the roof, and gave custody to the city of San Antonio. The Daughters of the Republic of Texas (DRT)—many of whom were descendants of Alamo defenders—organized in 1891, with one of their objectives being the preservation of historic sites. This group

The Paseo del Alamo was constructed in 1981 to open a passageway from Alamo Plaza through the Hyatt Hotel to the main bend of the San Antonio River. During excavation, part of the original west wall of the Alamo was uncovered and can be seen at the entrance to the waterfall-lined walkway.

intervened in 1903 to prevent a syndicate from turning the Hugo and Schmeltzer building (the original barracks) into a hotel. By 1905, the state of Texas had purchased the barracks and the grounds and turned custody over to the DRT, which has since maintained and operated the entire Alamo compound at no cost to the taxpayers of Texas.

Meanwhile, the plaza in front of the old Alamo chapel developed into a center of city life. In 1859, German brewer William Menger opened his elegant hotel on the southeast corner of the plaza, and later, when the San Antonio Street Railway System began to carry passengers from Alamo Plaza to the lush picnic and amusement park at San Pedro Springs in 1878, much of the downtown commercial and outdoor market activity centered around the plaza.

Though the plaza has been arranged and rearranged over the years, the basic configuration has remained the same, with streets and a landscaped park occupying what was once the mission's courtyard.

The grounds of the Alamo include a number of newer buildings designed to blend in with the older historic structures.

The proceeds of the DRT's museum and souvenir shop support the upkeep of the Alamo compound. The DRT also maintains a meeting hall and extensive research library.

For visitors and newcomers interested in a comprehensive overview of San Antonio's history, the exhibits and slide show available in the Long Barrack at the Alamo are an excellent place to begin.

The Alamo chapel contains additional exhibits showing details of the battle. You can see the reconstructed rooms where the defenders made their last stand, along with a collection of memorabilia from the Battle of the Alamo and from the men who fought there. Included are such items as Davy Crockett's buckskin vest and rifle, the Bowie family knife, William Travis' estate records, flintlock rifles, maps, and paintings.

Like the scant remains of Mission San Antonio de Valero, these items can never tell the whole story of the mission-fort, but they bear witness to its long and varied past. The intimate details from the lives of the defenders and their families and from the Alamo itself stand as a symbol of those ideals that call for the ultimate sacrifice.

I know that river, it's my baby. They used to call me Old Man River." These words by Robert H. H. Hugman, concept architect of the San Antonio River Walk, were printed in the *San Antonio Light* newspaper on May 19, 1974, and he was right. The San Antonio River was his baby, and the River Walk, as we know it today, was his vision.

The story of the development of the San Antonio River Walk began with a natural disaster. In September 1921, the city experienced a severe flood. Heavy rains caused the river to overflow and cover large portions of the downtown sector. In some places, floodwaters measured eight to nine feet above street level. Lives were lost, and citizens were justifiably outraged. City of San Antonio government officials had no choice but to face the problem head-on. Hawley and Freese, an engineering firm, was hired to study the situation and make recommendations. Two of the firm's suggestions were approved and enacted, but two were not. One of the rejected ideas called for the river area we now refer to as the Paseo del Rio, or River Walk, to be converted into a thoroughfare. Losing the river did not appeal to the San Antonio Conservation Society and the City Federation of Women's Clubs. Not only did they stop this proposal, but they also suggested the river and its banks be preserved and transformed into a city park. Hugman shared their view.

Hugman, a native San Antonian, graduated in June 1924 from the School of Architecture and Design at the University of Texas in Austin. He spent the next three years living and working in New Orleans, where he witnessed the ongoing conservation and preservation program painstakingly administered in the Vieux Carré district. Upon returning to San Antonio in the spring of 1927, Hugman envisioned the same kind of effort being afforded the San Antonio River.

His objectives were to save the natural beauty of the setting; control flooding; add pedestrian walkways on both sides of the river; construct appropriate bridges and walkways over the waterway; and develop shops, restaurants, clubs, an outdoor theater, hotels, and urban living spaces along its banks.

To take his vision from drawing board to reality, Hugman met with the mayor, two city commissioners, property owners, and civic leaders on June 28, 1929. He spoke eloquently of his plan to turn the San Antonio River into a graceful, romantic, and historic centerpiece for the city. He evoked images of the shop-lined cobblestone streets in Spain and the gondola-filled waterways in Venice. His ideas met with favorable reaction, but the Great Depression made funding the project virtually impossible. Undaunted, he continued to promote the idea of river beautification at every opportunity.

Finally, on October 25, 1938, the city of San Antonio issued a $75,000 bond, endorsed by seventy-four of the seventy-six property owners and residents who owned or lived on property on either side of the river from Jefferson to Villita streets. Issuance of the bond opened the floodgates, so to speak, for securing a $355,000 federal grant through the Works Progress Administration (WPA). After almost ten years of living the dream, Hugman was officially hired as architect of the San Antonio River Beautification Project. What stands today as the San Antonio River Walk basically reflects his original concept and design. Sadly, after only seventeen months on the job, Hugman was relieved of his duties. As the story goes, he was informed by WPA bookkeepers that materials designated for use on the River Walk had been delivered and used at another project in the city. Hugman took the evidence provided to him by WPA personnel to a well-known city judge who was a member of the River Board. Almost immediately Hugman was

OPPOSITE PAGE: *A fully loaded river barge plies its way down the San Antonio River with the Tower of the Americas, the Lila Cockrell Theatre, and the Marriott River Walk Hotel in the background.*

fired. In doing right, he was wronged. The project was completed without him on March 14, 1941.

Today, the San Antonio River Walk has reached legendary status. The charm created by its cobblestone walkways, lush landscaping, and emerald-green waters is very real. Millions of people come each year to dine at sidewalk cafes, ride barges, and shop along the fabled riverbanks. Ernie Pyle, the well-known journalist of the 1940s, once described the San Antonio River Walk as "the American Venice," but an anonymous passerby may have said it best: "The River Walk is San Antonio."

ABOVE: *Rivercenter, a massive downtown shopping mall, features over seventy-five stores, a nine-screen AMC Theater, an IMAX Theater, Rivercenter Comedy Club, and a variety of restaurants. The 1,000-room Marriott Rivercenter Hotel is attached to the complex as well.*

OPPOSITE PAGE: *Casa Rio Mexican Restaurant was the first business to open its doors to the San Antonio River in 1946. This landmark establishment actually began canoe, gondola, and paddleboat rides that eventually evolved into the river barges of today.*

ABOVE LEFT: *Hundreds of thousands of fans witnessed a river parade celebrating the San Antonio Spurs' NBA Championship victories in 1999, 2003, 2005, and 2007. Tim Duncan is front and center here with the Larry O'Brien Championship Trophy.*

ABOVE RIGHT: *Strolling mariachis serenade outdoor café diners along the banks of the San Antonio River. The word mariachi refers to singing musicians usually dressed in silver-studded charro outfits with wide-brimmed hats. They play a variety of instruments, such as trumpets, guitars, violins, and basses.*

LEFT: *Adjacent to the River Walk on South Alamo between Commerce and Market streets stands the Torch of Friendship. Commissioned by the Association of Mexican Entrepreneurs of San Antonio and given as a gift to the city, the fifty-ton contemporary metal structure was created by well-known Mexican sculptor Sebastian.*

LEFT: *One of the favorite activities enjoyed by visitors is a barge ride along the San Antonio River. The ride itself is between thirty-five and forty minutes in length and is narrated by the boat driver. Each driver covers the same historical facts, but with his or her own personal twist. It's fun and informative.*

BELOW: *A barge ride on the San Antonio River covers a distance of two and a half miles. Riders can buy tickets and board at three locations: across the river from the Hilton Palacio del Rio Hotel at Market Street and South Alamo, at Rivercenter on Commerce Street at Bowie, and by the Holiday Inn River Walk at St. Mary's and College Street.*

ABOVE: *On the Friday after Thanksgiving, the mayor of San Antonio throws a switch, transforming the River Walk into a spectacular holiday display of colored lights. A festive river parade follows the lighting ceremony as thousands of onlookers line the banks of the river.*

OPPOSITE PAGE: *The Hilton Palacio del Rio Hotel, shown here during the holiday season, is the world's first modularly constructed building. Conceived by H. B. Zachry Company, The Hilton was completed in less than seven months in order to be ready for the opening of HemisFair '68.*

Neighborhoods & Architecture

San Antonio's rich architectural heritage has been crafted over the years by its many citizens—missionaries, Indians, Spanish and Mexican pioneers, settlers from the United States, and immigrants from all over the world.

The earliest San Antonio "neighborhoods" consisted of three independent, rival communities. In addition to the missions, two other groups established themselves in the San Antonio River Valley in the 1700s—the soldiers of the presidio and the small band of settlers from the Canary Islands who founded Villa San Fernando in 1731.

The Presidio de San Antonio de Béxar was organized in 1718, at the same time as Mission San Antonio de Valero. The mission was named "Valero" for the Viceroy of Mexico, while "Béxar" honored the Viceroy's brother, the Duke de Béjar or Béxar (pronounced "bear"). In later years, as the communities along the river grew and merged, Béxar came to describe the whole area around the headwaters of the river. Still later, the area surrounding and including San Antonio became Bexar County.

The presidio was established to protect and assist the missions and served as fort and home to the Spanish soldiers and their families. Recruited from the northern regions of Mexico (Coahuila, Saltillo, and Nuevo Leon), these frontierspeople were already accustomed to the hardships and isolation of wilderness existence.

The permanent location of the presidio was determined in 1722 by the Marques de San Miguel de Aguayo, the energetic and farsighted governor of Coahuila and Texas. He moved the presidio to a flat, fertile strip of land between San Pedro Creek and the big bend of the San Antonio River, both of which flowed vigorously in those days. The rivers provided irrigation as well as a natural line of defense against Indian attack, and the fields enclosed by the horseshoe bend of the river afforded a rich and protected pasture for the garrison's horses. Commerce Street, which later bisected these fields, was known for some time as El Potrero, or the Horse Pasture.

A garrison of sorts was built with its west wall running along San Pedro Creek. In addition to defending the mission, the soldiers cleared land, dug *acequias* to irrigate the fields, planted crops, and built *jacals* (small dwellings consisting of walls of upright wooden poles chinked with mud or clay and roofs of thatch) for themselves and their families. The community that formed around the presidio consisted, in 1726, of over fifty families with a total of more than two hundred inhabitants. After their military service, many soldiers settled in the Villa San Fernando as civilians.

The year 1731 was one of upheaval for the two emergent communities of the San Antonio River Valley. On March 5, Missions Concepción, San Juan, and Espada moved into the area from East Texas. Four days later, a weary band of fifty-six arrived at Presidio de Béxar, having traveled from the Canary Islands under the auspices of the Spanish government for the purpose of becoming permanent settlers in New Spain. Expecting an established farming community, the Canary Islanders were shocked to find raw frontier, with much of the desirable land already claimed by the missions and the presidio dwellers. Open land to the west and north of town remained under the control of hostile Apaches for years to come.

The presidio and Missions San Antonio de Valero and San José had by then been in existence for over ten years. Engrossed in meeting daily requirements for food, shelter, and defense, the families of the presidio had made no legal claim to their lands.

OPPOSITE PAGE: *Designed by the twenty-seven-year-old James Riely Gordon in 1894, the Romanesque-style Bexar County Courthouse is a mammoth four-story structure built of native Texas granite and red sandstone.*

The Spanish Governor's Palace contained both public and private rooms. This family living room, located just behind the formal entrance area, opens to the bedrooms and to a semi-enclosed patio just before the main garden. Floors are made of huge flagstones; the ceiling beams are hand-hewn. Walls three feet thick and a deep roof of earth and gravel together with the wood-burning fireplace insulated the occupants from heat and cold.

When the Canary Islanders arrived armed with promises from the King of Spain and orders for the presidio captain concerning land distribution, the soldier-settlers suddenly found themselves divested of their irrigated fields and water rights. The *Isleños* ("Islanders"), as the Canary Islanders came to be known, also received a square of land between the presidio and the bend of the river. This square became their town and was named Villa San Fernando after the heir to the Spanish throne.

The three groups—missions, Canary Islanders, and presidio dwellers—attempted to remain separate and independent. Each competed with the others for water, farmland, and grazing rights. None encouraged marriage outside the group. But by the end of the eighteenth century, economic and social necessity together with intermarriage had brought the Canary Islanders, Mestizos, Indians, and Spanish together into one identifiable Tejano community of about two thousand. Community status began to be determined less by origins and more by economic success.

Unfortunately, except for the missions, few structures from the 1700s survive today. The buildings of Villa San Fernando may be long gone, but the basic blueprint of modern San Antonio dates back to those first Spanish settlers. A map from the 1700s depicts the important features of San Antonio; then, as now, Plaza de Armas (Military Plaza), Plaza de las Islas (Main Plaza), the U-shaped river bend, and Mission San Antonio de Valero (the Alamo) formed the underpinnings of the communities evolving between the two rivers.

In early San Antonio, the principal citizens lived around the plazas or within one or two blocks of them. These plazas were modeled after those of European cities, intended to contain fountains and activity centers and to function as the community gathering grounds. The plazas remained the focus of city life until the turn of the twentieth century brought the electric tram, the automobile, and the consequent flight to suburbia. Though downtown was no longer a residential area, the location of the city hall in the middle of Military Plaza,

the Bexar County Courthouse on the south side of Main Plaza, the rescue of the Alamo in 1906, and the revitalization of the river in the 1930s ensured the perpetuation of the original configuration. The renovation and redevelopment of Main Plaza as a pedestrian plaza in 2007 accentuates the historical roots of the plaza and reestablishes its connection to the river. After the Texas Revolution, immigrants from the United States and Europe, particularly Germany, began to arrive in San Antonio in substantial numbers; Anglo travelers in the mid-1800s wrote of how the styles of Europe, the Southern plantation, and New England were gradually replacing the Spanish character of the architecture. Flat roofs and adobe walls were giving way to two-story houses with pitched roofs and columned verandas. Front yards were taking the place of central courtyards.

The Spanish Governor's Palace, located on the west side of Plaza de Armas (Military Plaza), is the one remaining structure from the original Presidio de San Antonio de Béxar. Completed in 1749 and used as a residence and office by the presidial captain (but never the official residence of the governor), this simple but gracious building, with its flat roof, flagstone floors, arches, and walled garden, was restored to its original floor plan in 1929 after years of use as a school, bar, and tailor shop.

Plaza de Armas served as a military post, stockyard, and drill ground from 1722 until the advent of the Republic of Texas in 1836. From then on, as English place names were substituted for the customary Spanish, it became known as Military Plaza. In the 1840s, it was cleared of buildings and transformed into a municipal market and open-air restaurant.

Stephen Gould's 1882 *Alamo City Guide* advised visitors to "proceed at once to Military Plaza and see the Plaza Market, one of the distinctive features of San Antonio." Early photos capture a square teeming with village activity—wagon trains, chili stands, hay wagons, produce vendors, and customers milling everywhere. Vendors sold vegetables, eggs, butter, poultry, chili peppers, and even songbirds in wicker cages.

LEFT: *Located on the west side of Main Plaza, San Fernando Cathedral was originally the parish church of the Canary Islanders. The cornerstone of the first church on this site was laid in 1738, but it took twenty years to complete the building. The present cathedral, a Gothic Revival design, was erected around the original in 1868 and reopened in 1873.*

BELOW: *The simple exterior of the Spanish Governor's Palace, San Antonio's one remaining Spanish Colonial home, belies the elegance of the interior. Built in the mid-1700s, the palace contains ten rooms and a small loft with an extensive walled garden in the rear. The flags of France, Spain, Mexico, the Republic of Texas, the Confederacy, and the United States that fly in front of the Palace represent the six sovereignties that have laid claim to Texas since the seventeenth century.*

By the 1880s, the "chili queens" had become an integral part of plaza life. Journalist Frank Tolbert notes in his book *A Bowl of Red* that these young women arrived on the south side of the plaza at dusk, bringing tables, charcoal braziers, and their cooked chili in clay pots. They set up oilcloth-covered tables and stools for customers. A large ornate lamp with a colorful globe lit each table, and the pungent aroma of chili simmering over mesquite coals called plaza residents, wagon drivers, locals, and visitors to feast all night.

According to Tolbert and others, chili may well have originated in San Antonio, evolving from a dish invented by poor families to stretch small portions of costly meat into as many servings as possible. In any event, the chili queens continued to vend chili on one plaza or another until the 1940s, when health department regulations overwhelmed them.

In 1891, the character of the plaza changed forever when the white limestone, Renaissance-style city hall replaced the open area in its center. Although vendors of many nationalities continued to peddle their wares outside the new city hall, much of the colorful market life moved to Alamo Plaza and to the west, across San Pedro Creek, near the present location of Market Square.

Plaza de las Islas (or Main Plaza as it was called after independence), immediately to the east of Military Plaza, is the original Villa San Fernando, laid out by the fifty-six Canary Islanders who arrived in 1731. The majestic San Fernando Cathedral lies between Military Plaza and Main Plaza. The Islanders laid the cornerstone of the original cathedral in 1738 and finished the building just in time for the visiting Bishop of Guadalajara to confirm the first communion class twenty years later. Paintings and photos reveal a solid Mission-style structure whose dome could be seen miles away by travelers approaching the city from the east.

The new and larger Gothic-style cathedral was completed in 1873 and built around the outside of the original so that services would not be interrupted during construction. San Fernando has remained the parish of many San Antonians

The cornerstone for Little Church of La Villita was laid on March 2, 1879. It has been home to several denominations over the years and today is an active nondenominational church. One of its widely recognized activities is April's Starving Artist Show. It is also a favorite spot for small weddings.

who trace their ancestry to the Canary Islanders. Each year on March 9, a mass marks another anniversary of the 1731 arrival of these families.

The Bexar County Courthouse, commissioned in 1892 and built of red Texas granite and sandstone, creates a massive presence on the south side of the plaza. The courthouse, with its two towers—one seven stories high with a distinctive beehive spire—reflects the Romanesque style popular at the time.

The La Villita settlement, sometimes mistakenly identified as the first San Antonio settlement, can certainly be called one of San Antonio's early neighborhoods. It sprang up on mission land south of the Alamo, on a high bluff above the river and close to the best ford—today's Navarro Street. Originally serving as farm and grazing lands for Mission San Antonio de Valero, this area attracted families and individuals who were

LEFT: *La Villita was the site of General Santa Anna's cannon line during the Battle of the Alamo in 1836.*

BELOW: *Located on the high southside bank of the downtown bend of the San Antonio River and bounded on the east by South Alamo Street and the west by Navarro, the area known as La Villita once served as home to the Spanish soldiers stationed at Mission San Antonio de Valero. Today, its restored shops house arts and crafts vendors and its plazas function as a gathering place for celebration, most notably as the location of the Conservation Society's Night in Old San Antonio, held each spring during Fiesta Week.*

probably squatters living there without legal title. In 1803, soldiers garrisoned in the old Mission San Antonio de Valero began to move into the La Villita area. Until 1809, the area was known as the Pueblo de Valero and had its own mayor and government. At that time, Pueblo de Valero, Villa San Fernando, and the presidio and the old missions were joined together to become one town.

After a devastating flood in 1819 inundated the lower plaza areas where many of the town's elite citizens lived, the high bluffs of La Villita, which had protected its residents from the rising waters, attracted new development.

During the siege of the Alamo, some of Santa Anna's forces were entrenched just to the south of La Villita, on the present site of the Fairmont Hotel.

Most of the existing La Villita buildings were constructed between 1850 and 1900. Small, European-style cottages became interspersed with the Mexican *jacals* and adobes, and probably housed the working people of nineteenth-century San Antonio.

Under the auspices of Mayor Maury Maverick, the Villita Ordinance of 1939 established this area as an arts and crafts center. The National Youth Administration and the city provided the funds and labor for restoration.

Known today as the La Villita Historic Arts Village, it is bordered by Alamo, South Presa, Villita, and Nueva streets, and it features brick- and tile-paved streets, old homes containing shops and studios, restaurants, and a church. You can enter the area from Villita Street just south of the Hilton Hotel or from the River Walk by climbing the steps of the Arneson River Theatre. Inside you'll find plazas, meeting halls, historic buildings, and artists' studios and galleries with fine pottery, glass work, jewelry, and woven items on display. The village accommodates celebrations such as Night in Old San Antonio (the San Antonio Conservation Society's major Fiesta fundraiser), Fiesta Noche del Rio, and the lighting of the River Walk Christmas display. The nondenominational Little Church is a favorite for weddings as well as host of the Starving Artists' Show, an annual fundraiser.

San Antonio abounds with buildings and homes from the 1850s through the 1900s. Ranging in style and function from the simple dwellings of workers to the elegant Victorian homes of merchants and ranchers, from the ornate city hall and Gothic San Fernando Cathedral to the old German-English school, which survives as a conference center for the Plaza San Antonio Hotel, these are the buildings of the settlers and

The elegant Victorian home of the Edward Steves family, 509 King William Street, was completed around 1878 in the German district known at the time as "Sauerkraut Bend." Donated to the San Antonio Conservation Society in 1953 by the granddaughter of the original owner, the home is open to the public. Thirteen-inch limestone walls, imported mahogany and native walnut woodwork, gracious arches with pierced woodwork details across the porch, and rooms filled with Victorian antiques all make this home a special visit.

immigrants who arrived in San Antonio following the Texas Revolution.

Less than a half-mile to the south of La Villita lies the King William area, which was designated a city historic district in 1967. By the mid-1870s, German immigrants represented one-third of the city's population. Ernst Altgelt, a German surveyor and lawyer from Comfort, Texas, moved to San Antonio and planned an elegant community along the river. He laid out three streets parallel to the river south of town and five cross streets. The main avenue was named King William after Kaiser Wilhelm I of Prussia; the parallel streets bore the names of American presidents Washington and Madison.

King William Street was never more than a few blocks long, as C. H. Guenther's immovable Pioneer Flour Mills (now the oldest operating flour-milling operation in the United States) were located directly across the river. The Guenther House, originally the family home and later a storage area, has undergone renovation and now contains a café and gift shop; the upper floors, filled with beautiful antiques, are open to the public.

The aristocratic families of the city—so many of whom were of German origin that the area was known as Sauerkraut Bend—built their homes in the King William area in the late 1800s and early 1900s. A stroll through this quiet neighborhood allows you to savor the elegant details and delightful variety of

According to family legend, brewer Otto Koehler selected a hill on Laurel Heights Place overlooking the skyline of the city and his gold-domed Pearl Brewery with a definite purpose in mind for his house. Sitting on the porch of his palatial Victorian home, he could determine whether his employees were hard at work by the color of the smoke coming from the brewery's stacks. Built in 1901, the Koehler House measures over 12,000 square feet and is on grounds that take up a full city block. Deeded to the San Antonio College District in 1971, the building is now known as the Koehler Cultural Center.

the beautifully restored exteriors—cupolas, verandas, bay windows, wide arches, lacy wood, and iron work. Styles range from Italianate and Monterey Colonial to Gothic and Romanesque Revival.

You can find the headquarters of the San Antonio Conservation Society and its outstanding local history library in an Italianate villa at 107 King William Street, near the corner of South Saint Mary's Street. Ask for the group's walking tour and map brochure of the city.

Although the private homes in the King William area are not open to the public, you may enter the Steves Homestead (at 509 King William Street) for a small fee. Filled with antiques of the late nineteenth century, the interior of the home typifies elegant Victorian decor. It is owned and maintained by the San Antonio Conservation Society.

You will also find many lovely homes from the early twentieth century in neighborhoods such as Laurel Heights, Monte Vista (a National Historic District), Olmos Park, and Alamo Heights.

San Antonio has retained and reused a multitude of older buildings, thanks in good part to the efforts of the conservation society along with the interest and support of the community at large.

For example, the headquarters of H-E-B, a South Texas grocery chain, is located across the river from the King William area in a former U.S. Army arsenal, an active supply depot during the two world wars. The San Antonio Museum of Art on Jones Avenue resides in a reworked brewery, and the facade of the old Texas Theater has been incorporated into a modern bank building. Even the Johnson Street Bridge in the King William area had a former life as the first iron bridge built across the river on Commerce Street (1880).

The late 1990s saw the opening of the Alamo Quarry Market built on the grounds of the Alamo Cement Plant. Shops, restaurants, and theaters have been incorporated into the original buildings. The four giant smokestacks provide a focal point for the center and can be seen from miles away.

The French-designed limestone block and rammed earth (*pisé de terre´*) buildings of the Southwest School of Art and Craft, tucked away on a river bend just north of the city center, served from 1851 until 1965 as the Ursuline Convent and Academy for girls. Late in 1965, the prime riverfront property was rescued from high-rise development by the San Antonio Conservation Society. After some years, the Southwest School of Art and Craft began to occupy and restore the buildings with the help of the conservation society and local individuals who appreciated the beauty and history of the property. In 1998, a former Sears Automotive Center across the street from the original Ursuline site was retrofitted for studio and exhibition space.

Today, the buildings of the former girls' school house classes in weaving, pottery, photography, and papermaking, enrolling as many as five hundred students a semester. Visitors are welcome to view the galleries, shop in the gift store, and enjoy a simple lunch at the Copper Kitchen in the old refectory.

Across Augusta Street from the Southwest School of Art and Craft, you will see giant pink spheres poised to roll down the inclined plane that extends from the second floor of San Antonio's spectacular enchilada-red Central Library. Designed in the Mexican Modernist style by renowned Mexican architect Ricardo Legorreta, the building opened to the public in 1995.

On the north side of Alamo Plaza, the graceful, V-shaped Emily Morgan Hotel, with its Gothic-detailed upper floors, evolved from a former medical arts building. Cited as one of the finest examples of Gothic Revival architecture in the United States, it served for a long period as the site of doctors' offices and a hospital. Look closely for the terra cotta gargoyles hanging over the ground-floor windows. Do they not hint at toothaches and other medical maladies?

The various colleges and universities of San Antonio also feature historic buildings that have been lovingly preserved. The original Saint Mary's School for boys on College Street has been incorporated into La Mansion del Rio Hotel. The campus was later relocated to the far west side of the city and boasts an administration building designed by James Wahrenberger in 1894. Our Lady of the Lake University contains several magnificent Gothic Revival buildings from the early 1900s, also designed by Wahrenberger.

Brackenridge Villa on the University of the Incarnate Word campus sits on a wooded hill above the San Antonio River headwaters. George Brackenridge, a Scottish real estate mogul who owned much of what is today Brackenridge Park, University of the Incarnate Word, Fort Sam Houston, and Alamo Heights, purchased this land from Mayor J. R. Sweet and moved into the existing one-story homestead in 1869. As time and money allowed, he built a three-story Queen Anne structure as an addition to the original house.

A few years later, the Sisters of Charity of the Incarnate Word, founders of Christus Santa Rosa Hospital and Incarnate Word College, bought forty acres of the estate, including the villa. Today the restored villa is used by the college for offices and meeting space.

The red brick bell tower of the Incarnate Word Chapel, built to the east of the villa around 1900, is graced by four angels leaning confidently from each corner to sound their trumpets. Easy to miss as you pass down Broadway, the angels, along with hundreds of other engaging architectural details scattered throughout the city, reward the observant traveler or resident with clues to San Antonio's rich and lively past.

San Antonio College uses the Koehler Cultural Center at 310 West Ashby for studio and meeting space. Built in the early 1900s by brewer Otto Koehler, this ornate Victorian home was said to be situated high on a hill so that Koehler could sit on his front porch and observe the goings-on at his gold-domed Pearl Brewery some miles away.

Following Otto Koehler's death in 1914, his wife, Emma, became chief executive of the Pearl Brewery. She kept the business going through prohibition by producing near beer, bottling soft drinks, and moving into ice and dairy distribution. However, according to the Handbook of Texas, "within fifteen minutes of the end of prohibition in 1933, one hundred trucks and twenty-five boxcars loaded with Pearl Beer rolled out of the brewery grounds."

The twenty-two-acre site of the former Pearl Brewery itself is in the midst of a fascinating makeover. Located just a few miles north of downtown on the banks of the San Antonio River, the old brewery will soon house a beauty school, café, and culinary institute. The meticulously renovated Pearl Stable, once the grand home to the brewery's hard-working draft horses, provides an elegant event site.

San Antonians look forward to more exciting developments in what is planned as an urban village integrating education, cultural facilities, and fine food with residential and public spaces.

OPPOSITE PAGE, TOP LEFT: *The German-English School was established in 1858, and this building opened in La Villita around 1869. At that time, more than one-third of the population of San Antonio was German. Now owned by the Marriot Plaza Hotel, the building is used as a conference and event center.*

OPPOSITE PAGE, TOP RIGHT: *The Wulff House, now the headquarters of the San Antonio Conservation Society and its outstanding local history library, was built in 1870 by Anton Frederick Wulff, a German immigrant who settled in San Antonio in the 1850s. The three-story, Italianate-style house, which features random coursed ashlar limestone walls, a distinctive tower room, and a raised basement, stands at the entrance to King William Street.*

OPPOSITE PAGE BELOW: *The Kalteyer House at 425 King William Street is one of the few existing residential designs of James Riely Gordon, who was noted primarily as an architect of county courthouses.*

The "enchilada red" Central Library, designed by renowned Mexican architect Ricardo Legorreta and built on the site of the old Sears store, opened in 1995. Unique features of the library include a multistory, bright-yellow atrium graced by a twenty-six-foot glass Dale Chihuly sculpture and several outdoor plazas with landscaping and fountains. The northeastern facade features an inclined plane with huge descending spheres.

The cream-colored, James Wahrenberger–designed administration building of Saint Mary's University was built far out on the west side in 1894 to house the students of the overcrowded Saint Mary's College (located on the river where La Mansion del Rio Hotel now stands). Three French Brothers of the Society of Mary began their teaching efforts in 1882 in rooms over a livery stable on the west side of Military Plaza. Their determination and efforts blossomed into a 135-acre campus serving over four thousand graduate and undergraduate students. Here, thousands of San Antonians have received degrees in the liberal arts, business, and law.

LEFT: *Spire of the Gothic Conventual Chapel at Our Lady of the Lake University, designed by Leo M. J. Dielmann in 1923. The chapel is renowned for its spires, Italian marble altars, and German stained glass windows.*

BELOW: *The Gothic towers of Our Lady of the Lake University add interest to the skyline at 24th and Commerce streets on San Antonio's far west side. Founded by the Sisters of Divine Providence, OLLU provides a variety of programs and innovative scheduling options to the residents of San Antonio and South Texas.*

A trumpeting angel leans out from the tower of the motherhouse chapel on the Incarnate Word University campus.

The red-orange brick chapel of the Sisters of Charity of the Incarnate Word, built in 1907, overlooks the campus of Incarnate Word College on Broadway just north of Hildebrand. In the mid-1800s, three young women of this French teaching order arrived in San Antonio to assist during a cholera epidemic. These stalwart women founded two major San Antonio institutions: Incarnate Word College and Christus Santa Rosa Hospital.

Large Interior Form, *a sculpture by Sir Henry Moore on the Trinity University Coates Esplanade with the Murchison bell tower in the background. Designed to resemble an Italian Hill town and built in an abandoned rock quarry, the San Antonio campus of Trinity University opened in 1952.*

View south on St. Mary's Street toward the Tower Life Building. Built in 1929 as the Smith-Young Tower, it was the tallest building in San Antonio for sixty years. Its lighted green octagonal tower provides a distinctive look to the San Antonio skyline each night.

ABOVE: *The magnificent International and Great Northern Depot, designed by Harvey L. Page. Located at the end of Houston Street, the depot was built of compressed brick and stone and was completed in 1908. After years of disuse, it was restored in 1988 to a new life as the City Employees Federal Credit Union. Former ticket windows now serve as teller stations.*

LEFT: *The Italianate Victorian Fairmount Hotel, built in 1906, later attained* Guinness Book of Records *status as the world's most mobile building after its relocation from the corner of Bowie and Commerce streets to a spot five blocks away near La Villita. For four days in 1985, the city watched as the three-story brick building was jacked onto sixteen dollies and rolled slowly across the San Antonio River to its new location on South Alamo Street.*

Built in 1926 as a memorial to World War I veterans, Municipal Auditorium is a distinguished example of a Spanish Colonial Revival structure. Although a devastating fire in 1979 completely gutted the interior of the auditorium, the renovated and modernized building retains the stately elegance and grandeur of its origins.

OPPOSITE PAGE: *This Gothic Revival church was completed in 1898 to serve San Antonio's growing population of German Catholics. When church members declined to sell the building to make way for an expansion of Joske's Department Store in 1939, the department store was built around three sides of the church, leading to the local designation of St. Joseph's as St. Joske's.*

San Antonio is steeped in military tradition and history. From the Texas War of Independence in the 1800s, the names of Bowie, Crockett, Travis, and Bonham are etched in our memories. So should be the name of Robert E. Lee, who served in San Antonio as the Army Inspector General of Texas just prior to the Civil War. The famous Apache warrior Geronimo also spent time in the city at Post San Antonio, which later became Fort Sam Houston. His stay, however, was as a prisoner for forty days in 1886, confined to the watchtower in the Quadrangle while en route to exile at Fort Pickens in Florida.

Later in the century, the colorful Teddy Roosevelt formed and trained the First United States Volunteer Cavalry, better known as the Rough Riders, in San Antonio just prior to action in the Spanish-American War in 1898. And it is important to note that one of America's greatest military figures also called San Antonio home in the 1890s; Douglas MacArthur, whose father Arthur MacArthur was stationed at Fort Sam Houston, attended West Texas Military Institute through 1895.

The advent of the 1900s brought with it the first military airplane flight by an American, Lieutenant Benjamin D. Foulois, from the parade grounds at Fort Sam Houston on March 2, 1910. Foulois flew a Wright Brothers biplane for seven minutes at a maximum altitude of one hundred feet and a top speed of fifty miles per hour. John J. "Black Jack" Pershing used San Antonio as his expedition headquarters just prior to chasing the legendary Pancho Villa in Mexico before World War I. Army Lieutenant Dwight D. Eisenhower married Mary "Mamie" Geneva Doud while stationed in San Antonio. Lucky Lindy polished his skills here. So did Claire Chennault, later of Flying Tiger fame, and other daredevil aviators such as Frank Hawk, Jimmy Doolittle, and Billy Mitchell. San Antonio was in fact the "mother of the air force." At one time, in 1915,

San Antonio was home to the entire United States flying force, which consisted of six reconnaissance planes under the command of then-Captain Benjamin D. Foulois and was housed at the Fort Sam Houston Airdome.

After being promoted to the rank of major, Foulois was given the opportunity to select a site for a new aviation field in the San Antonio area. On November 21, 1916, he chose a large section of land five miles south of the downtown sector. Construction began in March 1917, and the first four planes landed there just over a month later on April 5, one day before the United States entered World War I. In June 1917, it was named Kelly Camp in honor of Lieutenant George E. M. Kelly, the first American military aviator to die in a military plane crash. Later the installation was called Kelly Field.

Also in 1917, an 873-acre site was chosen and ground was broken for still another flying field on the south side of the city. The U.S. Army eventually named this facility Brooks Field after Cadet Sidney J. Brooks, a native San Antonian who died in a flight-training crash at Kelly Field on November 13, 1917. The first airplanes flown at Brooks were the famous Curtiss JN-4s, commonly known as Jennies and used extensively in World War I. Sixteen hangars were constructed to house the flying fleet, with one remaining today. It's Hangar Nine, now used for the Edward H. White II Memorial Museum of space travel and flight medicine.

One of the most remarkable periods in the history of Brooks Field came between 1919 and 1922. Pilot training gave way to a balloon and airship school. A massive 91,000-square-foot balloon hangar was constructed for huge hydrogen-filled dirigibles. Both pilots and ground crew were trained at Brooks until several mishaps in operating the balloons caused the army to abandon the effort. After this, Brooks once again became a flying school

OPPOSITE PAGE: *The clock tower at Fort Sam Houston stands proudly at the quadrangle near the front gate of this fabled U.S. Army Base, now headquarters for the Army Medical Command.*

for the U.S. Army Air Corps and headquarters for the School of Aviation Medicine.

Other highlights in the early histories of Kelly and Brooks fields include the 1927 filming at Kelly of *Wings*, the only silent movie to ever receive an Oscar for best picture, and the first successful paratrooper drop in September 1929 at Brooks.

Fort Sam Houston, Kelly Field, and Brooks Field were followed by Randolph Field, dedicated on June 20, 1930, in San Antonio. Randolph was originally known as the "West Point of the air" because of its designation as the primary flight training wing for the U.S. Army Air Corps and later for the U.S. Air Force. Randolph Field was named after Captain William M. Randolph, an Austin native who earned recognition as a remarkable aviator in his eleven-year flying career. Of special interest at Randolph is the Taj Mahal, a 148-foot building-tower that originally served as administration headquarters for the base upon its opening in October 1931. The name comes from its slight resemblance to the shrine in India and from the tower's blue and gold mosaic dome.

The last of San Antonio's five military installations, Lackland Army Air Base, came on line in 1941. U.S. involvement in World War II gave Lackland its continuing role in training recruits. Throughout World War II, the Korean War, and the Vietnam War, Lackland trained millions of young men and women. Maybe this is why Lackland, later renamed Lackland Air Force Base, is still known today as the "gateway to the air force."

Three of these five major military installations continue operations in San Antonio today. Fort Sam Houston is headquarters for the Southern Command, which covers a fourteen-state territory. Brooke General Hospital, one of the largest military medical facilities in the world, is located here and specializes in the treatment of burns. The Academy of Health Sciences coordinates all army medical training in the United States from this base of operations. Randolph continues as home to Air Training Command, while Lackland remains the largest processing and training center for recruits and officer candidates in the U.S. Air Force. Its Wilford Hall Hospital is the largest of all U.S. Air Force medical facilities.

OPPOSITE PAGE: *Known as the Taj Mahal, this multipurpose building, designed by Atlee B. Ayres and his son Robert, opened at Randolph Air Force Base in 1931. It houses administrative offices, a 784-seat theater, and a water tank that holds 500,000 gallons. The Taj Mahal is 150 feet tall.*

This C-118 Liftmaster is one of the vintage planes at the static airplane display on the grounds of Lackland Air Force Base. To visit the display, you need a sponsor with a valid military ID.

BELOW: *The static airplane display at Lackland Air Force Base offers the opportunity to see a variety of planes from different eras, including World War II, the Korean War, Vietnam, and current day.*

ABOVE: *Lackland air force Base is known as the gateway to the U.S. Air Force. As headquarters for the 737th Training Group, Lackland is the primary air force basic training site for young men and women beginning service to their country.*

Located at Brooks City-Base, Hanger 9 houses a wide variety of military artifacts, including one of the few remaining JN-4 "Jenny" aircrafts from World War I.

This memorial to Vietnam veterans, known as Hill 881, is located immediately in front of Municipal Auditorium in the downtown sector. Dedicated in 1986, it depicts a medic attending to a fallen soldier.

San Antonio offers a variety of museums with permanent exhibits of traditional and contemporary art, regional history, popular culture, and natural sciences. The city's parks run the gamut—from the picnic-table, merry-go-round variety to a botanical center devoted to the cultivation and study of exotic and indigenous plants. The zoo exhibits animals from all around the world. These institutions engage in a mix of educational and outreach activities guaranteed to appeal to the interests of the community at large. Whether you're visiting San Antonio for a few days or have lived here a lifetime, you'll find a multitude of places to explore.

The San Antonio Museum of Art (SAMA) occupies the former Lone Star Brewery on Jones Avenue. Built in 1903 by Adolphus Busch of Saint Louis, the brewery was purchased in the early 1970s by the San Antonio Museum Association and transformed into an award-winning exhibit space.

For the most part, the exterior remains true to its original brewery design. However, architects reworked the interior into gallery space that is handsome and functional. A glassed-in catwalk connects two four-story towers overlooking the downtown San Antonio skyline on one side and the northern suburbs on the other. As they rise, the towers' glass elevators entice visitors with views of the exhibits on each floor.

Since opening in 1981, the San Antonio Museum of Art has become home to the region's finest display of Greek and Roman antiquities, Asian art, Latin American and folk art, and American paintings.

The Nelson A. Rockefeller Center for Latin American Art, a 30,000-square-foot wing dedicated to the study and appreciation of Latin American art, opened its doors in 1998. The Lenora

and Walter F. Brown Asian Art Wing opened in 2006. The museum's Asian art collections include more than 1,400 works from China, India, Japan, Korea, Nepal, Pakistan, Southeast Asia, Sri Lanka, and Tibet, spanning nearly 6,000 years of history.

On the east side of Brackenridge Park, you'll find the Witte Museum, featuring exhibits on South Texas history, culture, and natural science. Children especially enjoy the dinosaur exhibit and wildlife dioramas. In addition, the newly renovated H-E-B Science Treehouse offers four levels of kid-friendly, hands-on experimentation with simple machines, lasers, sound, electricity, air, and weather.

This is the perfect place to focus on what lives in and around a river, since the Witte is located on the banks of the San Antonio River. A new permanent installation continues the water focus begun by the popular World of Water exhibit presented during 2005.

In the water works area is a two-story concrete treehouse, created by Carlos Cortes to simulate wood. The treehouse overlooks the San Antonio River and is connected to the main H-E-B Science Treehouse by elevated walkways. Outdoor water exhibits feed directly from the San Antonio River and include an Archimedes screw, diversion gates, and water wheels. An underwater camera allows children to discover flora and fauna beneath the surface of the river, while the River Alive touch tank exhibits other tiny river invertebrates.

Four historic buildings from around San Antonio have been moved to the Witte's backyard. Three are used for staff offices, but the log cabin is open to the public. The Ruiz House was the home of the city's first schoolmaster, while the Twohig House

OPPOSITE PAGE: *Red and orange canna lilies outline the pool and fountain facing the main entrance of the Marion Koogler McNay Museum. Additions to the original three-story Spanish Colonial Revival–style house, built in 1927, have allowed the museum to expand and display its excellent collection, making it one of the finest small museums in the United States. The Jane and Arthur Stieren Center for Exhibitions will nearly double the size of the McNay and is scheduled to open in 2008.*

was built in 1841 by John Twohig, an Irish merchant whose store was located on Main Plaza. The Navarro House was built in 1835 by Jose Antonio Navarro, and the log cabin was constructed in 1939 by thirty youths participating in President Franklin D. Roosevelt's National Youth Administration program. The "dog trot"–style cabin represents the type of cabin built by many Texas pioneers.

The McNay Art Museum sits atop a hill at the corner of North New Braunfels Avenue and the Austin Highway, and it is surrounded by twenty-three acres of rolling landscaped gardens, sculptures, and fountains. Marion Koogler McNay bequeathed her Spanish Colonial Revival–style mansion, constructed in 1929, along with her extensive and important art collection of first-generation post-Impressionists and American watercolorists, to be used "for the advancement and enjoyment of modern art."

Since its founding in 1950, generous gifts from the community have enabled the museum to expand its collection and space. New galleries house permanent and changing exhibits. The Tobin Wing, opened in 1984, is home to the Tobin Collection of Theatre Arts, one of the premier collections of its kind in the country. In addition, the fine arts research library contains over thirty thousand volumes. The Leeper auditorium accommodates three hundred guests for lectures and receptions. The Jane and Arthur Stieren Center for Exhibitions, scheduled to open in 2008, will nearly double the McNay's floor space and allow it to host large, nationally renowned exhibitions.

Since 1985, the Blue Star Arts Complex, a sprawling warehouse area built in the 1920s for cold storage and located on the river not far from the King William area, has provided studio as well as exhibit space for contemporary artists. Contemporary Art Month, founded by the Blue Star, has grown to include over fifty collaborating organizations, cultural centers, museums, and alternative spaces. Within the four distinct gallery spaces at Blue Star, more than twenty exhibitions are showcased each year, highlighting emerging local, regional, national, and international artists and those

Housed in the historic, turn-of-the-century Lone Star Brewery, the San Antonio Museum of Art is home to the region's finest collection of Egyptian artifacts, Greek and Roman antiquities, Asian art, Latin American art, American and European paintings, and contemporary art.

who are internationally renowned.

Since 1995, the San Antonio Children's Museum on Houston Street has provided unique and innovative educational experiences for the youngsters of San Antonio. The museum has more than eighty hands-on, interactive exhibits that provide a wide variety of learning opportunities for children of all ages. Kids can enclose themselves in a giant bubble at the Hill Country Bubble Ranch, put on a hard hat and go to work driving a mini Holt front-end loader, or open a bank account and use a real ATM at the Good Cents Bank.

If your interests lean toward museums of the outdoor variety, take a picnic to one of San Antonio's parks, where you can view the impressive diversity of South Texas flora, examine exotic cacti and the trees of the tropical rain forest, or walk among an ever-expanding collection of the world's animal species.

In 1998, the San Antonio Museum of Art opened a new wing to house The Nelson A. Rockefeller Center for Latin American Art, the nation's only center dedicated to the exhibition and study of Latin American art.

San Pedro Park is the second-oldest municipal park in the United States—the Boston Commons being the oldest—and once contained the headwaters of San Pedro Creek. People have gathered around the springs and creek that originate here for some twelve thousand years. However, the land was formally set aside for community use by the King of Spain in 1734. During the late nineteenth century, this park was a popular picnic spot, although visitors risked being attacked by Comanches as late as 1860. San Pedro Springs Park was entered in the National Register of Historic Places in 1979.

Today, the park contains the McFarland Tennis Center, a branch library, and the San Pedro Park Playhouse, whose facade is a replica of the old Market House, razed in 1925. A renovation that lasted from 1998 to 2000 restored landscape and structural features that are important reminders of the park's long and interesting history. The beautiful swimming pool surrounded by enormous cypress trees remains a favorite cooling-off spot during the heat of summer.

Brackenridge Park, with its new main entrance at Broadway and Funston, may not be the city's largest park, but it's certainly the most popular. George Brackenridge, president of the Water Works Company and owner of much of the park's acreage, deeded a major part of it to the city in 1899. A $7 million renovation and redesign of the park was completed in July 2006. Most of the internal roadways have been converted to bike and walking paths. New play areas and picnic tables, several public art pieces, and improved lighting all serve to enhance the park's reputation as a favorite family gathering place for weekend picnics, birthday parties, and holidays such as Easter and the Fourth of July. To the delight of kids under age six, the miniature Brackenridge train still winds through the park, stopping at several stations along the way to allow riders to board or get off and explore.

The San Antonio Zoo, built into quarries from which the early Spaniards hauled stone for their houses, holds the third-largest collection of animals in the United States. The exhibit areas, built against the backdrop of the limestone cliffs of the abandoned quarries, simulate natural habitats wherever possible. Towering oaks, pecan, and cypress trees shade strollers in the heat of summer; the water running through the zoo is part of an irrigation ditch left over from the city's mission days.

HemisFair Park is the downtown site of the magical 1968 World's Fair, an event that brought the world to San Antonio's doorstep for a little while. During the fair's six months of operation, six million visitors flooded the city to see over ninety acres of exhibits housed in buildings constructed by citizens from twenty-five nations. HemisFair commemorated San Antonio's 250th year; to mark the twentieth anniversary of HemisFair in 1988, the city built a water park near the Tower of the Americas. Here, fountains, water cascades, and pools provide a refreshing stop on a warm San Antonio day. One of the most breathtaking views of the city can be found at the top of the tallest structure in the city, the 750-foot Tower of the Americas; the newly renovated restaurant and observation decks rotate once each hour.

The Institute of Texan Cultures, another permanent fixture of HemisFair Park, offers a rich insight into the diverse peoples of the state. Owned by the University of Texas, the museum aims to preserve and tell the stories of settlers from all over the world who made Texas their home. In addition to sponsoring the annual Texas Folklife Festival each June, the museum maintains a library, traveling exhibits and programs for schools, and an extensive photograph collection.

Part of a major urban renewal project, the clearing of the ninety acres for HemisFair destroyed many historic buildings. Others were saved and used as fair buildings. Exhibit halls built for the fair are now a familiar part of downtown San Antonio. Today, the HemisFair area contains the newly expanded convention center and concert hall, the National Autonomous University of Mexico, the Instituto Cultural Mexicano, an extension of Texas A&M Engineering School, and the renovated Beethoven Hall. The circular United States Pavilion became the John H. Wood Jr. United States Courthouse. In 1989 volunteers from all over the city generously provided design, materials, and construction for an innovative playground located in the southwest corner of the HemisFair area.

The San Antonio Botanical Gardens on the north side of the city off North New Braunfels Avenue offers thirty-three acres of exemplary Texas landscapes, as well as Japanese gardens (not to be confused with the Japanese Tea Gardens in Brackenridge Park), historic buildings, and a conservatory. Built on land that once belonged to the Brackenridge water-works and reservoir of the 1890s, the grounds are in a state of continuing development. An old-fashioned garden demonstrates the annuals and perennials used by Texas pioneers, while the Sacred Gardens reach back even further, displaying oleander, pomegranate, myrtle, fig, and other plants cultivated during biblical times.

Fifteen acres of land are devoted to native Texas plants representing three distinctly different vegetational regions of the state: the Hill Country, the East Texas Pineywoods, and the South Texas Plains. A one-acre xeriscape exhibit shows a variety of native and imported plants combined with irrigation techniques that use minimal amounts of water. The children's garden program enables children to grow and harvest vegetables from their own organic plots. The bermed greenhouses of the Lucille Halsell Conservatory complex grow tropical and desert plants of the New World; its one-half acre under glass makes it the largest conservatory in the Southwest. Other gardens include the Garden for the Blind, with highly textured plants identified by braille plaques, and the Japanese garden given by San Antonio's sister city—Kumamoto, Japan—as a gesture of friendship. The stone walks, ponds, waterfalls, and bamboo fences surround a copper-roofed teahouse where guests may sit and relax. Finally, the Sullivan Carriage House, moved one stone at a time from its original location at Broadway and Fourth streets, reflects architecture from the turn of the twentieth century. Its interior houses a gift shop, tearoom, and lecture hall.

SAMA houses one of the largest and most comprehensive collections of ancient Egyptian, Near Eastern, Greek, and Roman art in the southern United States.

Located in Brackenridge Park, the Witte Museum emphasizes South Texas history, culture, and natural science. Behind the museum, close to the San Antonio River, is the ever-popular, newly renovated H-E-B Science Treehouse, which features hands-on science activities for all ages.

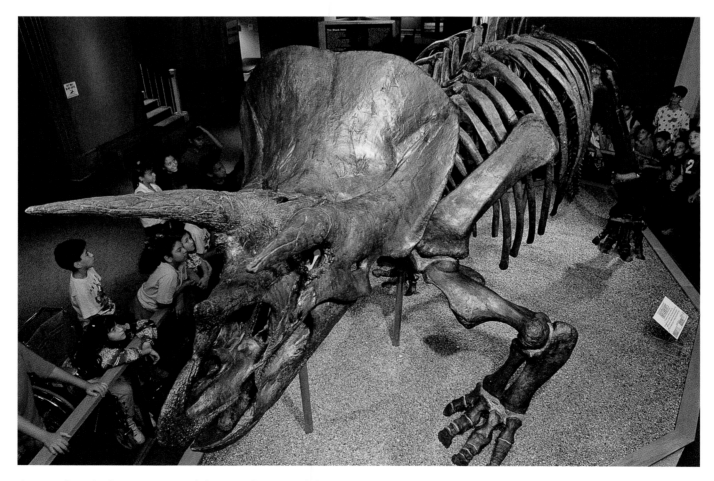

Among the Witte's permanent exhibits are dinosaur skeletons, cave drawings, and wildlife dioramas.

LEFT: *The Witte now includes an all-new, permanent installation to continue the water focus begun by the popular World of Water exhibit in the main gallery during 2005.*

BELOW: *Dedicated to inspiring lifelong learning through interactive play, the San Antonio Children's Museum is a fun place for kids ranging in age from two to twelve.*

The San Antonio Zoo and Aquarium, located in Brackenridge Park, is home to 3,500-plus animals representing 750 species, among them the endangered whooping crane.

Built to host the 1968 World's Fair, HemisFair Park has undergone many changes over the intervening years. Buildings such as The Tower of the Americas, the Institute of Mexican Culture, and UTSA's Institute of Texan Cultures still stand. The area now includes a water park and a children's playground, as well as the Texas A&M University Engineering Extension Service and the Universidad de Mexico.

Exhibits in this small museum focus on the Mexican and Mexican-American cultures. Recent exhibits include photographs by Mexican artists Lola and Manuel Bravo Alvarez, Juan Guzman, and others.

A replica of an 1863 Central Pacific Huntington steam engine pulls the one-fifth-scale model Brackenridge passenger train across a specially constructed bridge and over three miles of wooded and open area, crossing the river twice and allowing stops at four stations around the park.

Operated under the auspices of the City of San Antonio Parks and Recreation Department, the San Antonio Botanical Garden was founded in 1980 and encompasses thirty-three acres a few miles north of the downtown area. In addition to formal gardens, each of three Texas vegetative regions—the piney woods of East Texas, the plains of South Texas, and the Central Texas Hill Country—are represented by indigenous varieties of trees, soils, grasses, and plants.

OPPOSITE PAGE: *The San Antonio Botanical Garden's award-winning Lucile Halsell Conservatory has been specifically designed to shelter ferns, tropicals, palms, arctic plants, and other exotics from the debilitating heat and dryness of the South Texas climate. Tentlike glass pavilions extend sixteen feet underground where paths take visitors to the various exhibit rooms around the beautifully landscaped courtyard and pool.*

Entertainment & Festivals

The age of formal entertainment and performing arts in San Antonio really began in 1886 with the completion of the Grand Opera House on Alamo Plaza. This outstanding edifice was heralded as one of the finest performing arts venues in the nation at the time. Edwin Thomas Booth—brother of John Wilkes Booth, the infamous assassin of Abraham Lincoln—performed there. So did Sarah Bernhardt. Sadly, its existence was short-lived.

In April 1891, a lasting entertainment tradition was born in San Antonio: Fiesta. Women from the San Antonio Club decided to organize a parade to honor the heroes of the Alamo and San Jacinto, the battle in which Texas won its independence from Mexico in 1836. The parade was first scheduled for April 21, San Jacinto Day, but was changed to April 20 when the women learned President Benjamin Harrison would visit the Alamo City on that day. The theme of the event was the "Battle of Flowers," inspired by the flower carnivals of France and Mexico and the parades of Germany. But it rained on April 20, forcing postponement of the grand affair.

Even though the president had already left town, the parade, held four days later, was deemed an overwhelming success. Amid the pomp and dignity of bands, horsemen, floats, and carriages, parade participants actually threw flowers at each other. People were pelted, pelted back, and loved it. More than one hundred years later, the Battle of Flowers Parade is still the focal point of the ten-day celebration in April that we now call Fiesta San Antonio. Hundreds of thousands of people line the streets to catch a glimpse of flower-covered floats, marching bands, and kings, queens, and duchesses—royalty for the moment. Through the years, two more parades have been added to Fiesta: the Texas Cavaliers' River Parade and the Fiesta Flambeau Parade, both evening events.

Fiesta is food, fun, and celebration. It is a coming together of San Antonians and visitors alike. Many meet at NIOSA, A Night in Old San Antonio, held annually at La Villita. This four-night extravaganza features an array of food booths, music, dancing, games, and merriment. During peak hours, the volume of revelers overwhelms the area. A sea of people celebrates. It's part of the charm of NIOSA.

More than a hundred other events are held during the ten-day party at locations throughout the city. From 1891 to the present, Fiesta San Antonio has become one of the largest city celebrations in the United States.

The 1890s also brought San Antonio one of the most magnificent concert halls for musical and vocal performances in the Southwest. Beethoven Hall, located on South Alamo Street, was conceived, created, and completed in 1895 by the Beethoven Maennerchor, a German singing society. Unlike the Grand Opera House, which eventually was demolished, Beethoven Hall remains in use today.

The next great influence on entertainment in San Antonio came in the 1920s with the opening of two movie and vaudeville palaces. The Aztec Theater on Saint Mary's Street at Commerce opened in 1926, and the Majestic Theater on Houston Street, featuring a Moorish design by John Eberson, debuted in 1929. Both were large-capacity houses that featured silent movies and "talkies," as well as live stage performances. Today, the Aztec has been restored and features large-format films on a giant screen. The Majestic has also been restored to its original grandeur by Las Casas Foundation and is currently the home of the San Antonio Symphony, touring Broadway plays, and other performing arts events.

OPPOSITE PAGE: *For over a half century, the San Antonio Charro Association has continued the tradition of charreada (Mexican rodeo) in the Alamo City. Performances are held from March through September each year with a special Fiesta Charreada in April.*

The pageantry of the Battle of Flowers parade is greatly enhanced through the presence of these women on horseback wearing brightly colored dresses that depict the city's rich Spanish heritage.

Fiesta royalty, resplendent in a magnificent gown of many colors, greets onlookers from her float in the Battle of Flowers parade.

The Aztec and the Majestic weren't the only theaters of the era, just the most incredible ones. As a matter of fact, in the 1920s theaters lined the downtown streets. Their names seem symbolic of this golden age of entertainment: the Empire, the Palace, the Prince, the Bijou, the Strand, the State, the Texas, the Rialto, the Rivoli, and the Royal, to list a few. Regrettably, almost all of these entertainment houses are gone. Only the Empire remains. Adjacent to the Majestic, this small venue has also been restored by Las Casas. Fast-forwarding to the late 1940s, The Alameda Theater on Houston Street opened as the largest Spanish-language theater ever built in the United States. Its future is that of a restored Pan-Latino performing arts center in partnership with the Kennedy Center.

Another of the Alamo City's most-loved events had its beginning in March 1928. Originally called the International Exposition and Livestock Show, it is now known as San Antonio Stock Show and Rodeo, which occupies several weeks of our lives every February. After its completion in the late 1940s, the Joe & Harry Freeman Coliseum became the venue for this country and western showcase and remained so for over a half century. Today, the rodeo calls the AT&T Center home. Each year, all the real cowboys and cowgirls, and the drugstore kind too, show up to see top-notch entertainers, bucking broncos, snorting bulls, very fast clowns, the midway, and more. Probably more boots, hats, and western duds are sold to tinhorns during the thirty days leading up to the rodeo than during all other months of the year combined.

The San Antonio Symphony Society was next in the city's arts and entertainment future. Organized in September 1939, the symphony has provided San Antonio with many of its greatest classical and popular music moments. Its service to the performing arts patrons of the city has been extremely important through the years. An evening spent with the symphony in the atmospheric Majestic is magical.

And speaking of magic, when the sun rose over San Antonio on April 6, 1968, HemisFair '68—San Antonio's World's Fair—ushered in a new era for the city. Ninety-two

With skirts swirling, participants on this Battle of Flowers float perform a salute to Mexican dance.

acres of downtown property were transformed into a most colorful and festive exposition. San Antonio invited the peoples of the world to the party. And they came, by the millions. For HemisFair, the city built the Henry B. Gonzales Convention Center, HemisFair Arena, and the Lila Cockrell Theater for the Performing Arts. The convention center has been expanded several times in order to accommodate the growth of meetings and conferences that come to the city. In one of the expansions, it was necessary to remove HemisFair Arena, once home to the San Antonio Spurs. The Lila Cockrell Theater has been updated through the years and continues to host performing arts events such as opera, ballet, theatre, and individual performances. For the record, the San Antonio Spurs, many-time NBA champions, play their home games at the AT&T Center.

Fiesta, the rodeo, the symphony, HemisFair '68, and the Spurs have all made their impact on entertainment in San Antonio, as have Sea World, Six Flags Fiesta Texas, and the Texas Folklife Festival at the Institute of Texan Cultures. Held annually in June, the festival is a celebration featuring the arts, crafts, music, dancing, and lifestyles of the forty nationalities that settled Texas. Two other organizations that have contributed immensely to cultural growth of the city are the Carver Community Cultural Center and the Guadalupe Cultural Arts Center, representing the interests of the African-American and Hispanic communities of the city, respectively.

San Antonio is not only a city of fiestas; it's also a city of feasts! Although San Antonio is best known for its Mexican food, many other culinary influences exist. Diners throughout the city also enjoy the tasteful traditions of such peoples as the Germans, French, Italians, Polish, Greeks, Lebanese, and Asians. The palates of millions of annual visitors and locals alike savor the San Antonio culinary experience.

Nevertheless, Mexican food is royalty in San Antonio. The charm of the River Walk, the Alamo, and the missions lure people to the city, but it's the native food and fun that make them want to stay. While listening to the musical strains of mariachis, many experience a taco, tamale, or tostada for the first time. In fact, Mexican food as we know it in San Antonio may be America's best-kept culinary secret. We call it "Tex-Mex," a cuisine that has evolved through the years with both Texan and Mexican characteristics. You won't find it, in its purest form, in any state in the union except Texas, with San Antonio harboring its finest kitchens. Mexican food restaurants can be found in every area of the city, from the River Walk and El Mercado to hotels and downtown streets and from cozy corners and neighborhoods to malls and the expanses of suburbia. If you are a visitor, sample and savor at one, two, or a few. If you are a native San Antonian or South Texan, continue your never-ending search for the absolute best.

Outstanding high school bands and dance teams are invited to march in the Battle of Flowers parade each year.

Riders on golden palominos proudly carry the colors of our nation in the Battle of Flowers parade.

OPPOSITE PAGE: *King Antonio is showered with confetti as he rides on his royal float in the Texas Cavaliers River Parade. Throngs of people crowd the banks of the San Antonio River each year to witness this unique event.*

The Aztec Theater opened in 1926 originally showcasing vaudeville and silent movies. It remained an atmospheric movie palace until its closing in 1989. In 2006, the theater reopened after being totally restored by Euro-Alamo Management, Inc. It now shows large-format films on a massive iWERKS screen.

The fully restored lobby of the Aztec Theater is home to a spectacular, million-dollar special-effects show every ninety minutes that is free and open to the public.

LEFT: *The rodeo clown is a bull rider's best friend. In recent years, rodeo clowns have become known as bullfighters, a most appropriate description for this group of fearless men.*

BELOW: *The San Antonio Stock Show and Rodeo takes center stage every February at the AT&T Center. Cowboys from all over North America compete in this two-week rodeo that is one of the largest in the country.*

ABOVE: *The festival, an annual event held in June on the grounds of UTSA's Institute of Texan Cultures at HemisFair Park, celebrates the rich heritages of forty ethnic groups that make up the cultural diversity of Texas.*

OPPOSITE PAGE: *Since 1972, the Texas Folklife Festival has provided the opportunity for cultures from across the state to showcase their traditional foods, music, dance, and crafts.*

TOP: *A young girl is all smiles in front of a cascarone booth at Night in Old San Antonio. A cascarone is an empty eggshell that is filled with confetti and brightly painted. Cracking them on the heads of unsuspecting people is the name of the game.*

BELOW: *Here is proof that a picture is worth a thousand words. Night in Old San Antonio, held over a four-night span at La Villita during Fiesta San Antonio, is a very popular event.*

OPPOSITE PAGE: *The Majestic Theatre, designed by famed architect John Eberson and opened in 1929, is home to the San Antonio Symphony and The Majestic Broadway Series. The theater also hosts many other live musical, dance, and comedy performances each year.*

LEFT: *Smokestacks from Alamo Cement Plant now form the centerpiece for Alamo Quarry Market, an open-air shopping, dining, and entertainment complex in the Alamo Heights area of the city.*

BELOW: *The Shops at La Cantera is a unique mall next to Six Flags Fiesta Texas with outdoor walkways that lead to many impressive inline stores, like Tiffany's, and large anchors such as Neiman Marcus, Nordstrom, Dillard's, and Macy's.*

The Rattler rollercoaster has been the enduring symbol of Six Flags Fiesta since the opening of the park in 1992.

Little ones enjoy a ride on the helicopter at Kiddie Park on Broadway. Opened in 1925, Kiddie Park is the oldest children's amusement park in America.

We have painted a portrait of San Antonio and its place in history. It is the Alamo City, the Cradle of Texas Liberty, the home of the River Walk, the mother of the U.S. Air Force, and one of America's four unique cities. The people who live here are proud of their city's heritage. The people who visit here are captivated by San Antonio's charm.

"*Solomente en San Antonio.*" From Fiesta San Antonio and the Texas Folklife Festival to the San Antonio Stock Show and Rodeo and the Tejano Conjunto Festival to any day of the year, San Antonio offers nonstop entertainment, food, and fun. San Antonio has character. It's a great place to visit but an even better place to live.

The King William Association throws its own party during Fiesta San Antonio. It's called King William Fair and includes a parade, ethnic foods, music, rides, and games.

OPPOSITE PAGE: *A river barge passes under the Commerce Street Bridge next to Casa Rio Mexican Restaurant. Holiday lights glisten in the trees above. The Hyatt Regency River Walk Hotel is in the background.*

Shown here is the skyline of San Antonio in the evening with the Tower of the Americas at left.

ABOUT THE AUTHORS

Susanna Nawrocki has been the general manager of the Twig Book Shop in San Antonio since 1976. A native of Akron, Ohio, Nawrocki arrived in San Antonio in 1974 steeped in Ohio history, and unable to tell the difference between a taco and a tamale. She and her co-author wrote this book with the intent of providing other newcomers and visitors with the introduction to San Antonio she looked for but could not find.

Gerald Lair has worked as an advertising consultant, freelance writer, and editor since 1970. Originally from Pearsall, sixty miles south of San Antonio, he has been a resident of the Alamo City for almost four decades.

ABOUT THE PHOTOGRAPHER

Mark Langford (left), a 1980 graduate of Brooks Photography Institute in Santa Barbara, California, has owned a photo illustration studio since 1984. His photographs have appeared nationally in advertisements, publications, brochures, and annual reports. Langford is a lifelong resident of San Antonio.